Change is possible.

In praise of OVERRIDE!

"*OVERRIDE!* is a hearty, full-bodied invitation and permission slip to question your status quo. Anne shares thoughtful and creative ways to help you discern what's true and right for you as a way of life."
—Natalie Lue, author of *The Joy of Saying No* and founder of *Baggage Reclaim*

"Wonderful! Immediately warm and endearing, then page-by-page helpful and applicable insights. The perfect bedside book for a daily read."
—Derek Sivers, author of *Hell Yeah or No* and *Anything You Want*

"This is a book that meets the moment. Anne delivers her urgent wake up call for creativity. You might well find yourself drawing your own future map on a banana in this playful handbook for explorers in waiting."
—David Pearl, founder of Street Wisdom and author of *Wanderful*

"A playful permission slip to go beyond the status quo. Any creative—or person who aspires to have more creativity in their life—will find lots of gems in this little book!"
—Jamie Varon, author of *Radically Content* and *Main Character Energy*

OVERRIDE!

A POCKET PLAYBOOK FOR POSSIBILITY

*WHAT IF THERE WAS
ANOTHER WAY?*

BY ANNE S. DITMEYER

ANOTHER
WAY
— PRESS —

OVERRIDE! What if there was another way?
A pocket playbook for possibility
© Anne S. Ditmeyer 2024
All rights reserved.

First edition.
Another Way Press

Cover design: Anne S. Ditmeyer
Interior design: Anne S. Ditmeyer
Illustrations: Anne S. Ditmeyer
Words: Anne S. Ditmeyer

ISBN print: 979-8-9900747-0-5
ISBN e-book: 979-8-9900747-1-2
ISBN audio book: 979-8-9900747-2-9

For bulk orders please visit: override-book.com

OVERRIDE! What if there was another way? A pocket playbook for possibility was 100% written and edited by humans. No AI was used in the creation of this book. (No judgment towards those who use AI, but writing this book was a reminder that sometimes things need to get messy as we work through it to get to the good stuff.) In a world that loves speed and instant gratification, *OVERRIDE!* is a playful invitation to dance with discomfort.

To G for being a spark, mirror, and puzzle piece for this book to unfold.

To LO for constantly thinking out loud with me as we detective the world.

To everyone who has been part of MYP and bold enough to share themselves—being you expands my vision endlessly.

And to my mom, who is guiding me in ways I'm still learning to understand.

Every year I reread The Alchemist *by Paulo Coelho, and every year it takes on new meaning for me. I hope that you will revisit this book in a similar vein, where every read-through leaves you with different insights, in different seasons of life.*

The breakdown.

WHAT IF THERE WAS ANOTHER WAY?

What if there was another way? / The uncommon choice. / How to use this book. / Engage your override engines. / Loading a new operating system ...

SETTING THE STAGE

Why is it so hard to override what we know? / Copy & paste without questioning. / Life is a journey. / An incomplete list of what shapes us./ On bias and inherent privilege. / Societal norms. / The missing curriculum. / The standards we hold. / Unlearning the ways we've learned. / We've lost play. / Change is hard. / The power of the collective.

PART 1: A WORLD OF ILLUSIONS

Life is not linear. / Dance with discomfort. / Redefining success. / The role of and desire for control. / Stereotypes and representation. / Rigged systems. / There's no such thing as normal. / Invisible vs. visible./ Chronic systems. In need of update. / A culture of fixers. / Rethinking the imposters. / What leadership looks like. / Work and identity. / The need for external validation./ Dopamine of instant gratification./ Our relationship with time. / Resistance to less vs. more. / The speed of life. / Procrastination vs. percolation. / Burnout. / On loss. / An incomplete, unofficial list of that which is broken. / Banana map what's broken. / Space for reflection.

PART 2: AN EMPOWERED MIND

What if ... ? / Embrace the beginner's mind. / Ask more questions. / Listen. Really listen./ Logic + intuition. / Mind-body connection. / We are all mirrors. / How we respond. / The story I'm telling myself ... / Reframe the way you see things. / Watch your words. Flip the script. / Reprogram your brain. / Fixed vs. growth mindset. / Scarcity vs. abundance. / It's all a spectrum. / Zoom in. Zoom out. / Creative constraints. / Alternative narratives. / Everything is energy. / Begin anywhere. Start where you are. / Action breeds confidence.

PART 3: ACTION TO OVERRIDE

Look how far you've come!

EXPLORE

Follow your curiosity. / Journaling. / Go for a wander. / Head to nature./ Get outside of your everyday. / Prototype + make something! / Diversify your bookshelf.

CHANGE THE CHANNEL

Press pause. / Monitor your overwhelm meter. / Speak your truth. / Go back to the basics. / Breathe and meditate. / Take a bath/shower. / Create a playlist.

PRACTICE

Two things can be true at once. / Define terms. / Storyboard your stories. / Tap into your mind. / Create a new habit, practice, or ritual. / Ask for help. Accept help. / Practice gratitude. / Take small(er) steps. / Celebrate small wins.

SUPPORT YOURSELF

Talk to a professional. / Set boundaries. / Permission to say no. / Write your own permission slip. / Stop overcomplicating things. / Give yourself some credit. / Take a nap! / Connect with others. / Invite in MAGIC! / Draw your own override button.

CLOSING

Other ways. / There's always another way. / This is only the beginning.

RESOURCES

IN GRATITUDE

ABOUT THE AUTHOR

WHAT IF THERE WAS ANOTHER WAY?

There is more than meets the eye. There are possibilities beyond what you can see.

"Travel is not about where you go, but how you
see the world."
—ANNE DITMEYER, PRÊT À VOYAGER

What if there was another way?

NOTES TO SELF:

What if there was another way?

Dubbed "the quiet one" growing up, I never thought I'd be the one to shake things up. But here we are and I've had enough of more of the same. My mom once told me I was born with my own special gyroscope (my grandfather got us to the moon and back, but that's for another story). Later in life she told me I may have been shy but I was a quiet observer taking it all in.

I've done enough observing. Now it's time to share what I've learned in an attempt to shift the status quo. Nothing is going to change if we passively sit back and wait for it to happen, or for others to do the work for us. Action is required. The time is now.

OVERRIDE! is a small but mighty book that invites you to ask, "What if there was another way?" It's for those who want to rewrite the way things have always been done in favor of a way that supports us not only as individuals, but also for collective working for the greater good.

In order to do this we're going to take advantage of the fact that our brains are malleable and we can carve new pathways—in other words, we can change our beliefs.

This happens through reprogramming and rewriting (overriding!) old stories buried deep in our subconscious. Over time we'll clear the cobwebs and chip away at layers of outdated ways, making way for new, more empowered beliefs to take seed, positively influencing how we move through the world. It's a different way of operating that needs ongoing reinforcement in order to take hold.

Change, both within ourselves and in the world at large, does not happen overnight. It's not a flick of a switch. We first must notice old patterns that no longer support us in order to intentionally break away from them on the journey to a new path forward. It's a process over time. We can't wait for society to do the "right thing." We can start small. We're going for small steps for big change.

Reading this book does nothing unless you implement what you learn. Agency, intention, and aligned action are required. It may be clunky or uncomfortable at first, but that's how we change the game and learn to play in a broken world. We're rewiring the matrix, while bringing our own twist.

Playbooks aren't written with the intention that you'll make every move at once. You run different plays depending on the situation at hand. A playbook ensures you're ready for anything. *OVERRIDE!* is designed to take the pressure off.

The journey is not linear. It may even be messy at times. Leave any high-performing, type A, people-pleasing, perfectionist tendencies behind and stay open. Know every small, imperfect action adds up. It's never too late. Start small(er). Lower the stakes and do this for you. Believe in yourself, that you're deserving, and that there is another way.

Let discomfort be a clue that you're doing something right, not that something is wrong. Also, some changes may be far simpler than we think, so don't be afraid to experiment and PLAY with possibility. In a heavy world, doom and gloom can consume our attention, but in the pages that follow, joy, hope, ease, and lightness are some of our barometers for success. We must engage with the world around us in different ways in order to override.

Real change not only takes action, it takes believing that there *is* another way, even if we can't quite see how we're going to get there. Trust. Don't rush it. Care for yourself along the way. You can revisit *OVERRIDE!* whenever you need. In fact, it likely won't all sink in the first time through. Different aspects will resonate more in different seasons of life.

Your mindset will be key. Stay open. Allow this to be an iterative process and an evolution of improvement—on your terms—over time. Together let's move the needle forward.

There is another way.
Anything is possible.

The uncommon choice.

I was always a rule follower, but where was it getting me? I was trained to judge the trouble makers, but maybe they were onto something? I was convinced authority figures were always right and parents and teachers always knew what they were doing. (Ha! Everyone is figuring it out.)

With time and age, and living through a worldwide pandemic and social justice movements, I've come to see clearly that there's a different way of doing things that is far more exciting—and necessary—than what society tried to prescribe for me. Override is the remedy.

Yes, we need experts in their respective fields, but equally important, we need to start paying attention to lived experience and listening to the voices that systems have long silenced. It's not a teeter-totter. Everyone can rise up.

At some point in my story, I started to realize that people saw me differently. As the American who made her way in France (becoming French through starting my own business, not by being sponsored by a company or marrying in), I somehow had one leg up on defeating the odds by doing things differently. I also like to keep things real.

This wasn't just about moving countries and navigating French bureaucracy but discovering myself split between two cultures, allowing me to see that there were different ways of doing everything—for better, and for worse.

Even the university career coach and my grad school professors told me I wouldn't be able to stay in France after my studies. Fourteen-plus years later I'm still here, and even earned myself French citizenship. Every time they'd see me in the years following graduation I found a little pleasure in seeing their faces with a mix of surprise and confusion as they said, "You're still here." Yes—yes, I am.

I wasn't set on being right, winning, or staying in France at all costs so much as I was curious to see what was possible if I tried. (Having health care is nice too.) Perhaps this is my best example of learning what could happen when I pressed override—as if it's some invisible button not everyone is privy to—even when everyone around me told me something wasn't possible.

While I was just living my life I started to realize that my biggest successes were coming from actively NOT listening to others, but trusting myself and going forward anyway, even if my choices didn't make sense to those on the outside. Along my journey so many people told me *c'est pas possible*—it's not possible—particularly those in positions of "authority." Over time I let this naysaying be the guide and motivation I needed. I started to flip the script as if to say, "Thanks for the intel, I'll go see for myself."

A friend would tell me, "I know you love France, but you really love a challenge." I've come to discover that many of the best things in life are the rewards for doing the hard or scary thing. The more I worked on myself, the better life got and I became more resilient for whatever came next. As I navigated this path, I was both following my intuition and also breaking old patterns that no longer served me.

As I fully integrated lessons I learned, I was no longer faced with the same ones again. Of course new challenges emerged, but a new confidence came with each, reminding me I could handle anything that came my way. Confidence came through taking action, not waiting to feel confident before I took the first step.

Perhaps my natural-born stubbornness played an advantage. School trained me to get the right answer, but I knew life was more than getting a good grade on a test. Vulnerability researcher Brené Brown talks about shifting from being right to doing the right thing. Writing this book is part of my own exploration of what that means. It's also part of my own healing journey as I've learned to navigate the world in a way that feels true to me, learning to do things "my way" and the good things that come from that. It's rarely rewarded by instant gratification.

The earliest seeds of this book came in August 2020 over a bottle of wine with a new friend (it even had the working title *Everything Is Broken*). The common thread that emerged? Disillusionment. Wait, what? You feel that way too? I thought it was just me! Life can be so performative and rarely pans out like we expect, or were trained and told. Even those shoulds, musts, and supposed-tos are constructs. How have we been operating like this for so long without questioning it? Why do we feel this way? Sure, at times the heaviness of these realizations can be a downer and a wake-up call, but there was real comfort in knowing we were not alone in our thinking.

It took over a year to return to the book, the ideas itching to come out. As I worked on it, I found endless conversations with clients, friends, and strangers mirror back so much of what I was trying to say, helping me find clarity.

In that time I was gaining new intel into how people were really feeling and operating. During the pandemic (the ultimate "creative constraint"), I launched two workshops: Write Your Own Rules (to create your own guiding principles for life), which inspired Mapping Your Path (a three-month workshop with creative exercises and a community). I found myself creating what I wished existed in the world and in doing so I was giving participants permission to override what was no longer working. Each exchange deepened the themes in the pages that follow.

As your Chief Dot Connector, I've adopted my grandfather's mantra of "it should be fun" in all of my work. I've put my background in design to good use to present ideas for the biggest impact, and minimal overwhelm. My hope is that *OVERRIDE!* becomes a playground for you too.

How to use this book.

You probably want me to tell you exactly what to do as you embark on this adventure, but the journey is different for everyone. Your engagement in the process is essential if change is going to happen. We may have similar ways of moving through the world, but we also each have our own unique operating system.

There's no one way to read this book, just as there is no one way to do life. You may want to read through the book once and then go back to respond to the prompts and exercises, or dip in where you feel pulled (or feel resistance). Open to a random page any day for a reminder you may need to hear. Follow your curiosity. Stay open to new pathways and other ways.

This book is your playground. Don't be precious with it. Let it be loved. Mark it up. Annotate it. (If it's a library copy, leave a note for the next reader to uncover.) Use different-colored pens, highlighters, and sticky notes. Add your own insights and references along the way. Take pictures of your favorite pages. (You are welcome to share these with me if you tag @pretavoyager on social media.)

You may also want to start a journal where you capture your own reflections as you read and have more space for exercises. Revisit the prompts over time as your own understanding of the world shifts. Everything we're looking at is going to take repetition and reinforcement to truly sink in and become a new pathway.

Here's where we're headed:

Setting the stage invites you to place yourself in the themes of the book, exploring what has shaped you, what you believe, and where you are today.

Part 1: A world of illusion explores the context, influences, constructs, conditioning, and systems around us that keep us stuck and blocked. This is the section where everything feels broken, but you realize you are not alone. Seeing, acknowledging, and naming what's going on is part of our liberation. From here we can dream of another way.

Part 2: An empowered mind examines mindset and reframes that you'll be able to carry through the book—and life—with a more empowered way of thinking. The reframes will not only help open you to other ways of thinking and seeing the world but also help take the pressure off so actual change is possible.

Part 3: Action to override presents tangible tips, tools, tactics, exercises, and supports that allow us to take action (change isn't possible without action). Many are far simpler than you may think! The goal is to move beyond autopilot and integrate ways of being that support new possibilities.

There's a wealth of resources in the back of the book to further support you. I intentionally put them there to keep you from getting sucked into the rabbit hole of distraction or inaction. **We're looking to override, not overload.**

Prompts to ponder and exercises are sprinkled throughout the book along with "playground pages" to help you engage with the material. Set a timer for five minutes when you encounter the exercises. Put on a calming song. Don't over-think them. See what comes out. You may surprise yourself. Notice when something feels sticky. You can revisit it later. Engaging with the exercises is essential to override our default programing. We'll reinforce from multiple directions.

We were trained to think we need to have everything figured to get started and know where we're going. Knowing you've had enough of the status quo is enough to start. As you take action, clarity and next steps will be revealed. Trust that you'll know the next step when you get there. One step at a time. Let go of any expectations around timeline. This a lifetime of work as we free ourselves from what has been holding us back.

Your body is the best indicator light of where to explore next. Tune into visceral clues and how certain questions, concepts, or ideas land with you. Notice your skepticism, your judgments, your resistance, where you feel overwhelm.

Get curious about the resistance and what possibilities it may be blocking. Where do you feel peace vs. where do you feel triggered or defensive? Pay attention too if a certain theme keeps coming up in conversation or around you— this is also worth exploring.

The world provides a mirror of lessons we can learn from. Every time you unlock a level you'll feel the release in your body. Take your time. Be kind to yourself. This is not a race.

There may be times when you need to step away and take a break from certain ideas. That is not only allowed but also encouraged (this is true for life too). When the seeds are planted, clarity tends to happen once you stop thinking about it, like in the shower or on a walk.

You may find you have more questions than answers to start, or discover areas in your life where you want to invite change. Maybe you've never considered an alternate way. Maybe you never knew there was another way. Maybe you've been scared. Maybe you told yourself "this is how I am," or "this is how it has to be," or you never realized the system was broken. Maybe you didn't know where to start. Maybe you needed to know something was possible.

This book is designed to be pocket-sized and easily digestible, giving you space and time to think and reflect. It's not one more thing to read or do, so much as a reminder in your pocket when you're feeling blocked, things feel tough, or you need a boost. It's your reminder to keep going no matter what life throws your way. You hold the key within you, and this book seeks to help unlock that.

This book isn't based only on my own experiences. It's deeply inspired by years of facilitating creative workshops for schools, teams, and organizations, and witnessing participants inside my Mapping Your Path community. I've learned that the real impact comes when participants learn through doing and unlock their own insights.

As you work through this book, consider your own interpretation of the themes explored through your own perspective. My ideas are only the beginning. Hopefully they become a springboard for your own explorations.

Not all ideas may resonate with you, or you may find a different term or example resonates more with you than what I've provided—that's wonderful! The words I use resonate with me, they're not a doctrine. This book is not meant to convert you to a way of thinking. Nothing is etched in stone. It's designed to open up a dialogue and possibilities for you, and reframe what's hard and heavy as something that can be freeing. I want to get you thinking. While not inherently complicated, many of the concepts I share felt abstract to me at first, and only years later did they click. No one said simple was always easy.

You'll be invited to explore why you may have always operated a certain way or accepted a certain truth. It will help you have hard conversations in a challenging world. Ultimately it will invite you to consider how you're showing up in the world, and help you find a way forward for any challenge or block you may face. (I'm rooting for you!) Don't feel like you have to master everything. There's nothing to prove here. It's an ongoing exploration. The process may feel like a messy knot, but with time, patience, and effort over time each thread you uncover will make you feel lighter. I will be here as your guide, but as the reader, you must come to your own realizations and trust what your next small step is. Trust your intuition.

Note too that this book is not meant to be a replacement for mental health professionals. You may actually find a therapist just the support you need on this journey. I've found triangulating different perspectives that resonate with me along with journaling to be essential in unblocking, unlocking, healing, and getting to the next level. I find it amazing how new clarity and liberation in one area of life can directly impact another—in a good way.

You are not the only one questioning outdated ways. If we want to make real change, we can't stay in our silos. Please continue the conversation.

You may want to invite others to read along with you or start a book club. There's a facilitation guide available online at override-book.com if you want to gather a group to read and work through the book together, or join the conversation at override-book.com/conversation.

Engage your override engines.

Globally, override is a three-step process that corresponds to the three parts that follow.

1. SEE, ACKNOWLEDGE, AND NAME WHAT'S GOING ON.
Being able to name and acknowledge what is really happening on both an individual and societal level is essential to the way forward. It may be counter to how we were trained and how we operate. Remove any judgment. All you need to do is notice to start.

2. REFRAME. REWRITE AN OLD STORY IN A SUPPORTIVE WAY.
Shift outdated thoughts and beliefs into a more empowered mindset. The secret here is not to get stuck in mastery and perfection but allow the possibility of a better outcome.

3. TAKE ACTION: CHOOSE HOW YOU SHOW UP.
This is where you show yourself there's another way by implementing what you've learned through the aligned actions you take. Focus on yourself rather than trying to change others. This happens through small steps: practice, repetition, and reinforcement over time.

First, we must set the stage.

Loading a new operating system . . .

STILL LOADING . . .

In asking "What if there was another way?" *OVERRIDE!* invites doing things differently. It goes back to the computer that updates its operating system. The core hardware (us) remains the same, but the software (the way we operate) gets updated. This is more than a reboot. It's more than an upgrade. It's a total override.

Some people may confuse override with restart or reset—but these options only bring us back to where we started. The same patterns keep repeating. Similarly, "force quit" is when we have to quit something to do what it was supposed to do from the start. Override takes these functions a step further—it's a reset with a different result. A new action is required to achieve a different outcome. We're breaking out of our default operating systems in favor of one that makes things work better.

Theoretically, these overrides and system updates are improvements, but we all know from experience that sometimes these new ways of doing things can have a few glitches. Fast-forward to a couple months later, and everything has been ironed out. We've erased those frustrations from our memory. Despite the initial annoyances of updates, we now see the benefits of those hurdles.

Humans aren't computers; still, overriding is essential for our system update. We're reprogramming ourselves as we deprogram what no longer serves us. In the process we may very well discover ways we've been getting in our own way, inadvertently self-sabotaging progress, trusting the ways of others before trusting ourselves. We're learning to unhook our identities of who we were "supposed to be" and how we're "supposed to act" as we return to our internal guidance systems. It's as if to ask, "What lights you up?" rather than "What does society tell you you should do next?"

When it comes to override we must keep in mind that we use override all the time when we ignore our gut, and the deep knowing that something—or someone—isn't right for us. We ignore cues from our body that something is wrong, or burnout is imminent. Society has trained us to "be nice" and "power through at all costs"—in other words, we're trained to ignore ourselves. This is NOT the type of override we're going for. This is the old programming we're looking to let go of. Instead, we want to use override to support ourselves in the long term, which in turn benefits the world around us too.

It shouldn't have to be said, but in the world we live in it's necessary: override should be acted on with a spirit of love—for oneself, for others, for the planet.

Our systems are broken. Systemic issues will be harder to override, but in order for them to change we must believe there is another way. We can no longer operate out of fear or worry that we're not good enough or worthy. There are systems that have been operating under the same rules for too long. They were designed to keep certain people ahead over others. A lot of the time these systems work the way they do because they've always been this way, and also because no one has bothered to question them, or found the right way to override them. Sometimes they operate in a certain way because of their creators. Who were the decision makers, and who was in the room and included in the process?

We like things to feel comfortable and safe, but that can also keep us stuck. Even with our computer upgrades there can be fear of what will be on the other side, and worry that we won't understand how things function. Remember this on the challenging days—it's part of the initial hiccup of change.

Ultimately, the updates are for the best and help us in the long run. When we stop trusting ourselves and move through the world like lemmings within the systems around us, that's when we get into the most trouble, often feeling the most broken. Awareness comes before action and it is essential that we hold compassion for ourselves as there is a lot to process. Our self-awareness grows alongside the awareness of systemic injustices.

All of these updates help us evolve. Once past the initial

hurdles, it will be less a shock to the (nervous) system. The trick is finding a way to do this in a way that feels true to you.

In this updated operating system we're in the driver's seat of our lives. Yes, we can keep going the way we've always moved through the world (keep the status quo) OR we can shake things up (and press override for the greater good). Real change takes time, and over time every small step adds up. The waves of reverberation bring change.

Override is a muscle that you can flex—once you start, you won't want to stop. Once the first domino falls, more will tumble. Unlock yourself and find your magic in the process.

Rest assured this is a playbook. The process keeps things real and it will be fun! Stay curious and see where it takes you . . . Get ready to load your new operating system.

Are you ready?

PRESS THE BUTTON.

Setting
the stage

**Understand your role.
Plot where you stand.**

"Can you remember who you were, before the world told you who you should be?"
—CHARLES BUKOWSKI, POET

What if there was another way?

NOTES TO SELF:

Why is it so hard to override what we know?

As we grow up we are molded by our experiences and environments. We are raised to think there's a certain way things operate.

Later in life we find ourselves faced with a giant matrix of programming we must undo and move through. Until we open our awareness, we keep repeating what generations before us knew—the copy and paste of how things are done. If we want change, we must be intentional about it.

If we've only ever seen something done one way, we may never question it. Seeing is believing, but in the times we live in we may need to believe there is another way in order to open other possibilities. We need imagination and we can't let others talk us out of it.

PLAYGROUND! PORTRAIT

Draw a self-portrait of how you feel in the world today.
Leave perfectionist tendencies behind. All artistic abilities
welcome. Date it so you future you has a point of reference.

Copy & paste without questioning.

There's a whole lot of copy and pasting going on in the world, but sometimes what we're copying isn't the best option, or the only option. We lose sight of who we are because we're too busy going through the motions of trying to be someone else, or doing what works for someone else.

This even happens when people are launching a new website. They may look to a competitor and do the same thing. The thing is when you copy what's on the outside, you don't have a full understanding of what's going on behind the scenes on the inside, or if it's even working.

When we copy and paste we perpetuate more of the same. The patterns get repeated, even the dark patterns. Sometimes patterns can be supportive, but they may keep us stuck. The same is true for our individual selves.

And while it's true we don't need to reinvent the wheel, what is important is to remember to weave in and integrate our own story or twist so we're not perpetuating more of the same.

PONDER:
What is getting repeated in your life without questioning?

Life is a journey.

Override is a practice of many things, including letting go of perfectionism, which keeps us stuck in the same loops. Overambition can often get the best of us, and guilt builds as time passes if we haven't achieved our goal. Let's avoid self-combustion. Don't be so hard on yourself. Don't attempt to override everything at once. Practice imperfection.

Allow this process to be messy. (Life is messy!) Go for progress over perfection. Many people resist "the work," fearing what lies ahead and what it may reveal, or prefer to stay happy in their zone of comfort. I operate by the mantra "rock the boat, or the boat will rock you." Neither is particularly fun, but the latter is far more destabilizing, so we may as well make sure it's on our terms. Doing the hard thing is worth it in the long run.

You are not broken. You're not a failure. You're not behind. You're just human. The sooner that you can accept that, the easier it is to move forward. Also know you're not the only one who feels like this.

None of this is as heavy or as hard as it sounds when you take it in stride. Being bold can be trying something that feels scary, but once you try it you realize it's not so bad. The journey involves both stretching yourself to try new things and paying attention to how we may be in our own way or holding ourselves back.

What if anything worth doing was messy? No one said things feeling messy is a bad thing. It's just life. Enjoy the process. It's a journey of discovery.

Take these questions forward with you to ponder:
+ *Why do I believe the things I believe? (Around work, how things happen, relationships, the world.)*
+ *What keeps getting repeated in my life without questioning? Where do I want to invite change?*
+ *What would it look like if I did things my way? In a way that feels true to me?*
+ *What if the journey was fun? What if it were easy? How is it counter to how I was taught?*
+ *What if small shifts over time make the biggest difference?*
+ *How do I want to feel? Do I believe I'm worthy of feeling that way?*

An incomplete list of what shapes us.

Why do you believe what you believe? When we cross experience with context and environment we start to uncover the nuance of life and the belief systems that influence our behaviors and inform our actions.

So much of the world around us shapes us: parents, caregivers, neighbors, friends, random comments from strangers, teachers, school, religion, places we've lived (urban vs. suburban vs. rural), experiences, language, laws, wealth and means, class, privilege, skin color, ethnicity, sexual orientation, medical history, access to healthcare, education, accessibility, disability, mobility, body type, mental health, exposure to other cultures and places, trauma, grief, stigma, shame, etc.

The work of Bruce Lipton explores how most of our belief systems get programmed into our subconscious from an early age (age 0–7). No matter how good our childhood was, our inner child (and potentially a wounded one) is running the show more than we realize. Addressing our inner child is also where our biggest healing can occur later in life.

Social media in particular can make it far too easy to tell

ourselves stories about what someone else's experience is like. We tend to see/share the highlight reel of life, exuding confidence, yet as the viewer it's all too easy to project our own ideas of the reality of others. Really, we have no idea what's going on. But our own insecurities and feelings of inadequacy build. On another level it may show us clues to what we're really craving in our own lives.

We may never know the full story, and we weren't wired to admit hardship. I was born in the early 80s, part of a generation that lacked the awareness around emotions that younger people have, which is even more disparate from the relationship with emotions that my parents' generation had. We're simultaneously learning and unlearning while imbibing false realities. Vulnerability and honesty are powerful tools for connection—with others and ourselves.

Family and marriage therapist Vienna Pharaon, author of *The Origins of You*, acknowledges that the "presenting problem" clients bring is rarely the actual issue they're facing. When we look to our origins (past) to understand why we've been operating in a certain way, we can start to heal. A specific event, challenging time, or offhand unsupportive comment from someone we respect may have affected how we move through the world. We can start to see why we—and the world—operate the way we do. What has served as a protective mechanism in the past may no longer serve us moving forward. It's time to disrupt the pattern.

PRACTICE:

One of my favorite go-to tools is mindmapping. It allows us to think in a nonlinear way where we can see connections between ideas that we may have otherwise missed.

Create your own mindmap of influences. Start with you at the center (name or portrait). You may want to explore your family, location, or environment (where you grew up), the role of religion, friends, and people you spent a lot of time with, school, cultural upbringing, and any other factors that have shaped who you are today.

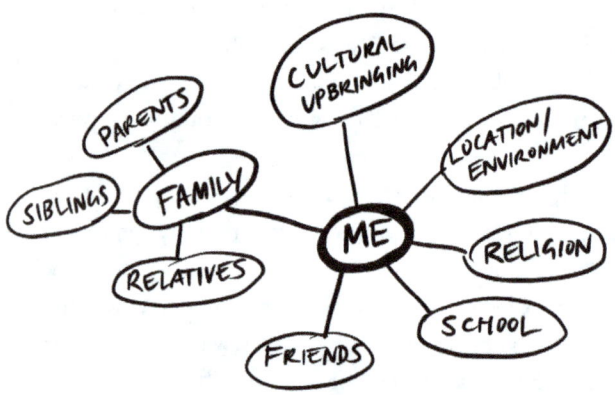

This mindmap is just the base framework. Keep adding spokes, branches, and offshoots with more detailed information, factors, experiences, and influences to explore each idea deeper, as well as the beliefs you hold. We're looking for insights, not a work of art. (You can find my expanded mindmap at **override-book.com/conversation**.)

PLAYGROUND! MINDMAP

Draw your mindmap of influences. Share it with a friend to facilitate a conversation.

On bias and inherent privilege.

Truth-telling is a key ingredient if we're going to override any of these old, outdated ideas and systems holding us—and society—back from a better, more humane world. This starts by accepting your own truth (often the hardest part). You may be amazed by what happens when you do! This also may mean accepting that imperfect action and making mistakes (and learning from them) are part of the journey.

The ideas and themes explored in this book emerged from my own journey and perspective as a white, cisgender, able-bodied, child-free woman born in the '80s who grew up in the US (DC, Minnesota, Kansas, Idaho, Virginia, and Maryland, if you're curious) and now lives in Paris, France. Each location has shaped my experience, along with my travels and the people I've met along the way.

Note that many of the ideas and issues explored in the pages that follow may have a US-centric spin. You have my permission to adapt and question as needed according to your own life experience, wherever you're reading this book.

One cannot talk about overriding without acknowledging the privilege that comes with the ability to do things differently and to take risks, or the option to quit. There is privilege in gender, race/skin color, means/access/financial stability/backing, access to healthcare/mental health/childcare, education/experience, upbringing—the list goes on.

Depending on how we grew up, we may never have considered how others navigate the world, or how we may be subconsciously judging others without understanding their own life experiences and challenges.

I grew up thinking that a diploma from a top-rated university was essential for success, a message I absorbed from the world around me. Now I've come to see that some of the most successful people I know didn't go to university, and others who did are held back or are unhappy because those accolades that validated them along the way aren't playing out like they expected in the "real world" although they followed the "perfect" path laid out for them. We all have the power to learn from each other when we override.

PONDER:

What factors have helped shape your view of yourself, or how you view the world around you? What opportunities and access do you have that others don't have access to?

What biases and inherent privilege do you carry with you? (Refer to your mindmap for more ideas, and update it too.)

PLAYGROUND!

What narratives did you grow up with? (True or not.)

Societal norms.

If you asked your childhood self what you imagined life would look like, the standard path might look something like this:

SCHOOL > UNIVERSITY > GET A JOB > FALL IN LOVE > GET MARRIED > START A FAMILY > RETIRE > LIVE HAPPILY EVER AFTER

Add the adjective "good" in front of most of the categories (e.g., a "good job") and congratulations, you're an upstanding citizen! But what makes a job good and by whose standards? If it's a popular brand that gets great press and pays well, but they treat you like crap or it's a toxic work environment, is that still a good job? How many of those "good jobs" that we applaud are actually with corporations destroying the planet? We must ask what we actually value.

And what if you didn't get a diploma? Does that make you less educated? Learning can come in many forms. We tend to underestimate lived experience and what can be learned on the job and through life. Would you rather have someone on your team who is curious and eager to learn, or the know-it-all who was at the top of their class and doesn't feel like they need to listen to anyone else?

Society is particular in how it assigns value. We don't always know how to handle or respond to those who haven't taken the preconceived path. What, you don't want to sit behind a desk all day every day so you can earn a pension? Marriage isn't your #1 priority? You don't have/want kids? You haven't done X by a certain age? You're actually excited to get older and aren't afraid of aging?

None of this makes you a freak of nature. Absorbing unintentional judgment through the questions of others can make us feel less than or broken, in addition to the stories we tell ourselves. Our brains cling to the negatives rather than the good stuff. These beliefs often become subconscious blocks in our brain (they're locked away deeper than we realize) that need our attention to clear pathways to change.

Society isn't always comfortable with "unconventional" ways of doing things, but that's not your problem. Engaging override also involves learning to trust yourself even if your life doesn't fit into the prescribed societal blueprint. We must let go of caring what others think.

Keep going!

The missing curriculum.

It wasn't until my late thirties that I started to realize I needed to do work on myself. Life hadn't unfolded quite like I expected. Things were going fine enough, especially on paper—I had moved to Paris (the "dream!"—at least for some) and started my own business. However, I remained disillusioned by the fact that in all my schooling—which included two master's degrees by this point—no one had ever given me an indication that self-work was the real "work."

To be honest I felt pretty blindsided. As someone who sees myself as an intelligent being, how could I miss this memo?

All those Advanced Placement classes didn't translate to much in the creative/professional path I took. I took all those classes not out of interest or desire, but because I was told they'd look good on paper, to help me to get into a good school. In high school I had no clue what I wanted to do, or the full range of possibilities out there.

What I would have loved in school was an emotional education. Even years into therapy I don't always have the vocabulary to describe an experience, let alone emotions. My childhood catchphrases became "I don't know" or "I don't care" (in the sense that I thought not having an opinion was helpful—it wasn't!).

To be honest, part of it was just the nature of growing up, but I also don't think I fully knew I was allowed to have an opinion and take up space as a woman, and I cared too much about what others thought. Because I was so good at going through the motions of life and being an upstanding citizen, it took some time to learn to be honest with my therapist (ahem, with myself) about what wasn't working and how I was really feeling and to chip away and get clear on what I truly wanted in life.

School is good at testing tangible outputs, but I've learned that my biggest successes come from that which is intangible, and often invisible—namely following the crazy ideas that pop into my head that may not make sense to anyone else. This is definitely NOT what I learned in school.

Looking back, I really wish school emphasized curiosity rather than right answers. I also would have loved a personal finance course and learning how to file my taxes, but those systems benefit from us not knowing too.

PONDER:
What do you wish you had learned in school? Or in life?
#thingsiwishilearnedinschool

The standards we hold.

Throughout school there's more emphasis on learning for the test (it's measurable) than learning for the sake of learning. So much of our experience depends on the teacher. The teacher has limitations and is guided by standards of curriculum and material that must be covered. (If we look at how we value teachers, that says even more about the systems we live in.)

Standards are a good thing, but it's also important to recognize that they may have limits. Many of our well-meaning intentions (and systems) have a dark side. I was a straight-A student in high school, with unimpressive SAT scores. My standardized test scores were not good for my ego, or comparison with my friends. Yet somehow I knew that a standardized test did not define me (and I fortunately got accepted to a top public university).

Sure, I could have spent more time (and my parents' money) on SAT prep classes. Did that appeal to me? Not in the slightest. I somehow knew there was a different path for me that did not involve filling in bubbles of multiple-choice questions. **There's always another way.**

Unlearning the ways we've learned.

School—at least in the US—teaches us that we need to have a robust résumé if we want to get into a top college. We need sports, we need clubs, we need volunteer time, we need leadership positions. We are trained to do this throughout our existence, and we must do it all to look good, to be successful. (Hello, privilege!)

Teaching in traditional universities was challenging for me when students were more concerned with how to get a good grade than learning or exploring the material. We are trained to think that accomplishment and accolades equate to happiness, and that being tired and busy is a badge of honor. Is this really the badge you want to wear?

We've come to equate doing all the things as a prerequisite for success. We think the validation of someone else's approval is a sign that we're doing life right. Here's the thing we don't question: What if all that doing is actually getting in the way rather than helping us? Are we even headed in the right direction?

On top of it we put arbitrary timelines and expectations on when and how things should happen, from jobs to love, health, and healing. There is disillusionment and disappointment when it doesn't happen when we think it should. We can feel more broken than we already did. One way of living may be what we need for one stage of life, and that's fine, but people can also grow out of it. We all make these realizations at different times, on our own time.

I've found the frame of seasons far more supportive than thinking about timelines, and some seasons are fallow in order to allow future growth. School won't teach you this, but it's never too late, and there's no such thing as behind. Take the timelines off everything.

There are so many great things that you learn in school too, but education doesn't only take place in the classroom. I wouldn't be where I'm at without the podcasts, books, and unofficial education in my life. Learning doesn't stop when school ends. It's a lifetime adventure.

PONDER:

What's one important lesson you learned outside of school?

We've lost play.

How do you learn best? We must be "serious" to be an adult—but says who? Have you ever noticed how much kids play vs. adults? Kids are constantly asking questions, curious about the world around them.

School starts out fun, with lots of play, and is very tactile. It's how we learn. The older we get, the more play gets removed in favor of rigid structure and tests. By the time we get to working age, play is almost completely gone. Anything that doesn't resemble "serious work" gets cut from budgets. Whoever decreed "let's sit in chairs behind a screen all day!?!" Is that really how we make progress?

Play is harder to measure than standardized test results, but that doesn't mean it's not essential and valuable in our operations. Play and creativity make learning memorable. Play is an essential ingredient in the override process because it disrupts how we think the world needs to work. We can come up with creative solutions thanks to play.

PONDER:
How will you PLAY today?

PLAYGROUND! EMBRACE YOUR INNER CHILD

Do something that you loved doing as a kid without worrying what others may think. Crayons, markers, construction paper, origami, bubbles, baking cookies, playing hide-and-seek, or putting your favorite childhood song on to jam along to—it's all fair game. Unplug from this page and actually do it.

Doodle the kid-like activities you have reengaged with below. Create a list of things you want to do too.

Change is hard.

Change takes time. Even when we know we want to move on/forward, there can be a certain comfort in our old ways of operating (even when we don't want them). Moving into the new and coming into our own is always a little scary. Change takes courage. It's a process to rewire our ways.

Change doesn't happen as a flick of a switch, but rather plot points that evolve over time. That's why it's helpful to have markers in life as a frame of reference and to write things down so we can see how far we've come. Think of it as an upward spiral of expansion.

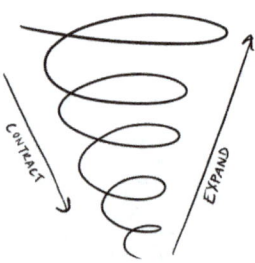

Don't judge where you are now. Be aware when you may be comparing yourself to others. We never know the full story of the lives of others. Be where you are.

In storytelling there is an "inciting incident" that sets everything in motion. In life, for some people the wake-up call is a single event—a rock bottom—and for others it's gradual, where a pattern keeps repeating over time in such a way that we know something needs to change or we may self-combust. Still, this is scary.

There is risk involved and we're not trained to normalize discomfort or that "failure" that can teach us lessons along the way. It may even take decades to see how the skills we've developed and experiences we've had over the years can help us in unexpected ways later.

We must remember change is possible and worth the effort. Think of an artichoke. You have to get through some spiky bits to truly get to the heart of it. We're shedding layers we no longer need.

Tara Mohr's book *Playing Big* is what helped me see fear differently. She addresses two types of fear that get named in the Hebrew Bible: *pachad* (a projected fear of what may happen) and *yirah* (the fear of stepping into something new or bigger than us). With *OVERRIDE!* we're stepping into something bigger. This is your reminder not to run and hide from fear but to step through it. Deep down we may even fear success, or that things may work out better than we could imagine.

What would happen if we said, "Hello, fear. I see you, and I'm going to keep going anyway"?

The power of the collective.

We all inspire each other in ways we'll never fully know. Sparks are ignited and spread between us, often in unexpected ways.

Before we can override the collective, we need to start with ourselves, but nothing needs to be mastered or "fixed" (you are not broken) for progress to take hold. It is through ongoing conversation, dialogue, and exchange that we can learn from each other, realize we're not alone, and unlock possibilities together. As you interact with friends and strangers, ask them questions inspired by themes in this book as a way to learn about their own life experiences.

Just like a virus can spread around the world, the hope with *OVERRIDE!* is that it's contagion for the greater good. Along the way, we can inspire each other with new ways of thinking, and showing each other what's possible.

It's time to rethink what we know, how we *think* change needs to happen, and who leads the way. We can be the heroes of our own journey. And those journeys may not look like we thought they would.

It's going to take the power of the collective to override the systems at play, and it all starts with one small action to override how things have always been done in our own lives. It may sound scary or daunting at first until we take the time to empower ourselves—not sit back and wait for someone else to empower us. This often happens at the edge of our comfort zones.

It's OK if it means we're figuring it out as we go. We just need to take the first step. By picking up this book, you already have.

During the World Wide Wander, a global event encouraging people to find answers in the world around them, Street Wisdom founder David Pearl shared the idea: "If we imagine better futures there's no guarantee they'll happen, but if we don't imagine them, they won't."

What if we allowed ourselves to dream a better future was available? Another way was possible? What if we believed we could be part of the change and make a positive impact? How will you show up now that you know you're an active agent of change?

Each small action you take will set off a chain reaction of dominos of change. Why wait to set things in motion?

PLAYGROUND! REPEATING PATTERNS

What keeps happening in your life that you're ready to let go of? Where do you keep getting blocked? What feels frustrating or scary that you can't quite move past? Write or draw it below as a reminder for future you.

PART 1:
A world of illusions

Familial, community, societal, and global beliefs shape our experiences—and point us to areas we may need to override in our personal lives.

"Systems of oppression, inequality, and inequity are by design. Therefore they can be redesigned."

—CREATIVE REACTION LAB

What if there was another way?

NOTES TO SELF:

Life is not linear.

When things go wrong, we're often caught off guard—as if life is supposed to be perfectly packaged and wrapped with a bow. Life is not always easy. We forget to stop and acknowledge that life is messy, life is raw, we can't control the news. In other words, life is life. It's anything but linear. Forward is not always a straight line.

While life can get us down at times, we also can look for the lessons between the lines with time. I like to invite the challenges as gifts that help redirect me. Things don't always make sense when we're in them, but later on we can see how it really was a detour in the right direction (a very Stoic way of thinking: the obstacle is the way).

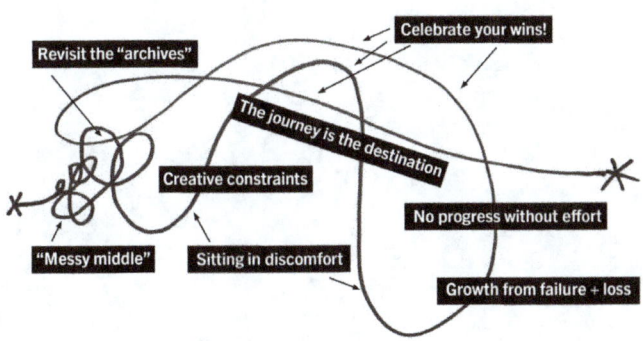

There's a learning curve to life as with anything. We make our way through the "messy middle." We make progress through effort. We return to what we know. The journey is the destination. Celebrate yourself and your wins along the way!

Clinical psychologist and ordained minister Dr. Thema Bryant reminds us in *Homecoming: Healing Trauma to Reclaim Your Authentic Self* that "The ultimate goal is not ultimately to return to who you were before encountering roadblocks, but actually grow in the aftermath of those detours and challenges."

PLAYGROUND!

Draw a squiggly line without overthinking it. Annotate it as your line of life. Include turning points and key moments.

Dance with discomfort.

Growth isn't always neat and tidy. The discomfort of transformation is real. Growth doesn't always feel comfortable and cozy. If only someone had warned me this was a reality of life. Yet it is often during the slow or in-between moments that the biggest growth happens.

We're so eager to hear about success stories that often the hardships get brushed under the rug. It's less glamorous, yet still present.

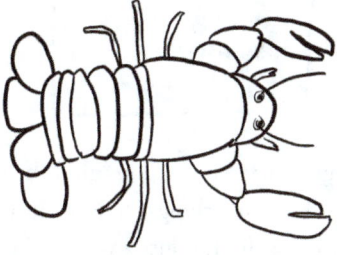

My favorite growth analogy is one I learned from a friend who shared the YouTube video "How Does a Lobster Grow?" with me. Dr. Abraham Twerski talks about how, just as a lobster or crab must grow into a bigger shell, when we outgrow our old ways, we too shed a layer that leads to one that's more fitting. It can take some time to truly feel at ease in our own skin, but we grow through adversity.

We don't always have the words to describe when we're "in it." For me the discomfort feels like I'm "in the goo." I try to remember a butterfly in a chrysalis state. Other times our minds may understand what's happening from a logical or rational standpoint, but often our bodies (and nervous system) have some catching up to do. We are updating our operating systems when this happens. We're stretching.

Discomfort can be a signal that you are doing something right. We can't escape it, so we may as well dance with it. Inspired by my friend Anna, I have a sticky note on my desk that says "I'm uncomfortable = I'm growing."

This is also why we need to keep in mind the timelines in which we tend to *think* things should happen vs. the reality of the process. It's not just a weekend or "when I get through X [event/deadline], I'll feel like myself again."

PRACTICE:

Draw or journal about discomfort you've experienced or worked through in the past. Let it be a reminder to your future self that you've navigated uncertainty and made it through (and can do it again).

Redefining success.

How do we see success as a society? How do we measure success? How much is external? How much is internal? In business we look at growth metrics, number of users/customers, money earned, etc. The graph is expected to move up and to the right steadily. It's as if constant growth is the only vision we can hold.

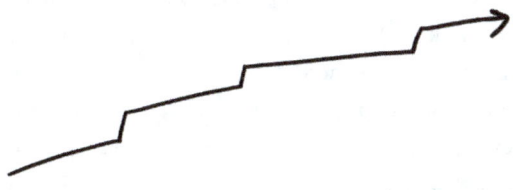

We can feel confused, frustrated, and even broken when that line of success doesn't look like we expected. Really, ups and downs are natural, with learnings along the way. It's how we grow and evolve. There are gaps in our expectations.

It's fascinating to look at billionaires as an example of "success." Society at large and the media praise exorbitant amounts of money as the pinnacle of success and assume we all should desire the same thing in life, or that money equals happiness. Yet billionaires never seem to be satisfied. There is never "enough"—they keep going for more.

It's a reminder of the illusion of assuming once we get to a certain level, we'll be happy and have everything we want. Their race to the top is never-ending; there is no "arriving."

Self-worth gets tied to success, output, and external factors in our operating system. We are born worthy, but it gets wired out through ways we think we need to move through the world to be appreciated or loved. We think we need to prove ourselves to others, but what if we don't? What if success was an inside job, not at all linked to your external accolades or financial metrics?

What if feeling and intuition were stronger than strategy in terms of getting real results? Society (and capitalism) makes us think we have to operate in a certain way. We rarely pause to realize success can mean so many other things too—joy, happiness, presence, harmony, etc. Where is the conversation about values when it comes to success? How are we elevating others?

PRACTICE:
What was the view or vision of success you had growing up? Rewrite, refine, or draw your current definition of success. Revisit and revise as needed.

The role of and desire for control.

We go through life thinking that we're in control. Hahaha-hahahahhaha! Look at your own life events and see what's happened and ask yourself how much you were actually in control. We're guilty of trying to control our own lives and outcomes, while also being inside a swirl of systems designed to control. No wonder life can feel like whiplash at times.

Control is an attempt to feel a sense of security in a world rife with uncertainty. We may not be aware, but control is all around us. Often our actions are our attempt to control, whether it's workaholism, perfectionism, diet (what we eat or don't allow ourselves), exercise, or planning.

There are so many decisions in the world that are made through the lens of control, but it's masked as something else. Particularly controlling others. From workplace rules designed to support certain people (and not others) to the right to vote, which is actively made more complicated in many historically underrepresented communities, control can look many different ways. In places like the US, there are many attempts to control women's bodies.

Control is power. However, used wrong, control is employed to keep some people ahead and others behind. It's often used to dim voices and quiet any other way. The invisible nature of control can make us question what we know when we're on the receiving end.

We can start to question more things, like who controls the wealth? Who controls decision-making? How do they represent the audience? We can continue to ask more questions for each question we answer. What if there was another way? Another paradigm? Another way to present the issue?

When thinking about control, we also can't forget to consider how we may be subconsciously trying to control a situation in hopes of a particular outcome. In a challenging world it can be hard to trust, but in some cases it's the missing ingredient. Change and growth will take as much time as they need to take. We're not always in control, and that's OK. When we try to force or control things, we often make things harder on ourselves. Instead, the journey through discomfort happens when we allow things to flow.

PONDER:

Where in your life does control show up? What do you want to practice letting go of? What happens when we remove attachment to outcome?

Stereotypes and representation.

If you look back to your childhood, who and what did you see represented on TV and in movies and books? What were the storylines about? What did they show you about what life would look like? Work? Friendships? Romantic relationships? Financial realities? Aging?

Do the jokes that were funny then stand the test of time? Are these storylines and narratives ones you'd want to be passed along to your children? Are you able to articulate aspects of what you grew up with as problematic? Can you see how you absorbed certain "truths" as fact?

How did the messaging shape your belief system? Did you see anyone that looked like you? In what ways did you feel empowered? In what ways did you feel limited? How did narratives around who is successful shape your experience? Did you aspire to be like the people you saw? Did you even think it was possible for you?

PONDER:
Reflect on things you have consumed that you now see as problematic or limiting. This is not about cancel culture but seeing influences to deprogram.

Rigged systems.

The world was not designed to be an even playing field for all. Our world is not only broken, it's rigged, favoring certain people. While I'd sensed things were broken for a while, it took the Black Lives Matter movement in 2020 following the murder of George Floyd to wake me up to the depth of injustices and the prevalence of racism and how it has shaped the world we live in. (It should never have taken that long.)

As part of my own reeducation, I signed up for a webinar offered by Creative Reaction Lab entitled "How Design Thinking Protects White Supremacy." During it, they opened my eyes to the broken systems and lack of equity. They shared work from Tema Okun's 1999 paper "White Supremacy Culture" [the three-page paper is available at whitesupremacyculture.info], which breaks down the characteristics of white supremacy:

– Perfectionism
– A sense of urgency
– Defensiveness
– Quantity over quality
– Worship of the written word

– Only one right way
– Paternalism
– Either/or thinking
– Power hoarding
– Fear of open conflict
– I'm the only one
– Progress is bigger, more
– Objectivity
– Right to comfort

These characteristics can be a warning light to do things differently and an invitation to show up and act in another way. This work made me aware of my own need to hit override now more than ever and is only one small fraction of what needs to be redesigned in our world. The injustices that have been baked into history must be undone.

Intersectionality further reveals the interconnected nature of categorizations such as race, class, gender, sexual orientation, religious affiliation, and body type to grant access, dominance, and value to some people over others. We can't put blinders on. This world is not an even playing field unless we actively change it. I acknowledge that I'm still learning, and I hope you will too. There are additional resources under "social justice" in the back of the book.

PONDER:
What systems of supremacy have you witnessed in or around your life? What actions can you take to educate yourself and override systems of [white] supremacy?

There's no such thing as normal.

A friend in her late thirties once told me, "I always thought I was broken. It turns out my brain works differently." For her, it was an ADHD diagnosis that was a liberating discovery allowing her to move past feeling "less than" and inadequate. Another time, a stranger told me that the world was not designed for her with autism, which got me thinking that I'm not sure the way the world was designed actually supports most of us.

Societal systems tend to operate under the assumption that everyone is the same, but that's not the case. We are not one size fits all. Society has learned to dictate standards for operation that keep us all in line rather than showing us a spectrum of possibilities where we can all thrive and contribute in our own ways.

Naming and acknowledging the range of experiences is key to our ability to override moving forward. What if we could accept that there is no such thing as normal?

PONDER:
Do you feel like you "fit in" or do you feel like an outlier?

Invisible vs. visible.

We're so used to operating by things that are visible, we can't always see experiences different than our own.

Here's an incomplete list of things that we rarely can see and are not talked about openly:

- Disability (wheelchairs and crutches are visible, but not all disabilities are: cognitive, mental, emotional)
- Chronic illness (brain injury, diabetes, cancer, long COVID, immunocompromisation)
- Neurodiversity (autism spectrum, ADHD, etc.)
- Depression and anxiety
- Caregiving (taking care of others, children, aging, sick)
- Grief (loss of loved one, loss of pet, loss of job, loss of life you thought you would live)
- Addiction (alcohol, drugs, shopping, gambling, scrolling)
- Financial pressures (debt, job loss, bankruptcy)
- Being human (headaches/migraines, menstrual cycles, allergies, recovery, responsibilities, loneliness)

There can be so much shame around any of these topics that they affect the way we operate in the world. Some people are more inclined than others to live their journeys out loud.

If you are going through life without any of these invisible aspects, there's a good chance you're moving through life with a certain amount of privilege (or denial). This is not to judge you. It's more to point out that many people do not have that luxury, and rarely will anyone advocate for them.

Are you able to go to work whenever you want? Leave whenever you want? Plow through deadlines or extended work periods without having to figure in any other factors (child or elder care, headaches, pain, accessibility, etc.)? Workplaces and school systems tend to be designed for a certain type of person to succeed. Even with additional supports in place, it's another layer for partners/parents/caregivers to manage and coordinate—who is taking that on? It's not a paid job. In fact, it's an exhausting one.

Unless there is someone close to us in life navigating an "invisible journey," we risk lacking empathy, understanding, and compassion for their experience.

PONDER:

What are factors others can't see that shape your experience?
What invisible factors shape people that you know?

Chronic systems. In need of update.

While we can feel frustrated in life, what if we could see we're not the issue? What if the way the world was designed is the real thing in need of overriding?

There are many people who silently take the brunt of the burden, whether it's someone with chronic illness who is told "but you don't look sick," or someone running a household or caring for others. Without an understanding of what's really happening, we may feel frustrated by their behavior or seeming inaction on the outside.

Spoon theory became popularized by the chronic illness community to describe the amount of physical and/or mental energy that a person has available for daily activities and tasks. Anything you do, including the unexpected curveballs in a day, takes a spoon from your already limited supply. Everything we do takes bandwidth—this is true for everyone, yet we all struggle to admit it.

Those with chronic illness or going through medical ordeals spend time waiting for appointments and bills while not feeling like themselves. On top of everything, they have limited capacity to focus energy and attention towards actual healing. It's hard. It sucks. Most people around you don't get it. Read the writing of Kate Bowler (*No Cure for Being Human*) or Suleika Jaouad (*Between Two Kingdoms* and *The Isolation Journals*) for an honest look at living with chronic illness.

In the neurodivergent world, there's a concept called "scaffolding" that provides temporary structure and assistance to help kids (or anyone) in specific areas and is then taken down when they've achieved their goal in that area. It's another concept we could all benefit from: offer extra support when you need it and take it away when you no longer do.

There are so many opportunities to learn from individuals and communities who operate in ways outside of the mainstream to inspire another way. Not only that, in the process they'll feel more seen.

PONDER:
How have you been inspired by someone who operates differently than the mainstream narrative, or how the world was designed?

A culture of fixers.

"When someone shares something with you, try not to immediately get into solution based advice, fixing it, interjecting your experiences. Try to let it be silent for a minute. Listen for the beauty or horror of the words. You cannot solve everything. This is not a bad thing."
—The Nap Ministry (Twitter, 27 Sept 2022)

One of the challenges we face as a society is that we are doers and we are fixers. We're not good at sitting in the in-between liminal space. We can end up contorting or giving up part(s) of ourselves because we're afraid to make other people feel uncomfortable in our efforts to make things better.

But what if the other person doesn't need fixing? Often we need someone to listen and to acknowledge it's hard or say "that sucks" and sit with you. We don't need advice, we need to be heard. What if we acknowledged that life isn't always comfortable? Full stop. What if we could learn to sit in the discomfort?

We rush to fix, to make better, to improve, but are there moments where we can just be? You can't change people, and you can't control others or the outcomes of their lives. On a societal and global level, especially when it's a cause that's close to your heart, chances are there are already activists on the ground doing the work. Don't try to be the savior. See how you can lend a hand, add your support, make a financial contribution, or spread the word. Don't underestimate the expertise of those who have a deep first-hand understanding of the issue, especially if they're from the population directly affected.

There are ways to do your part without having to fix everyone and everything. Often it starts with looking inward to focus on yourself and how you show up. You can lead by example and work on yourself. Do what lights *you* up and brings out *your* best self. Don't do it with an ulterior motive, do it for you. Ultimately, we need to care for ourselves first if we're going to be able to support others.

PONDER:
Instead of trying to fix or change someone else, what might you examine in your own life?

PRACTICE:
Learn to hold space for others where you practice being fully present and withholding judgment. Listen rather than trying to provide any advice, change, or fix anything/one.

Rethinking the imposters.

We may feel like an imposter or have been told we should feel like one. Our inner critics can be tough on us if we're not careful. Feeling like an imposter may include thoughts such as "I'm not good enough," or "I don't know what I'm doing."

When we internalize that being an imposter is a bad thing, it highlights all of our shortcomings and "failures." However, when we can recognize it's happening we can reframe this feeling through a more empowered lens, we can see the hurdle as something we can overcome. The more I observe certain "leaders" who are celebrated yet never question themselves, the more I can see through their performative nature, and I've come to see that feeling like an imposter is actually an asset. It means I'm not afraid to ask questions, challenge assumptions, and sit in discomfort.

The systems want to keep us small so it's up to us to take small actions to face the imposter. Part of this journey is finding deep self-belief within ourselves despite the noise of the world. Keep going anyway!

PONDER:
When have you felt like an imposter?

What leadership looks like.

Years ago, I attended a workshop called "Develop Your Authentic Leadership Style," hosted by The School of Life London, a "school" devoted to emotional education. When the facilitator, John-Paul Flintoff, asked us to list good leaders we've encountered in our life, I distinctly remember my mind going blank. Much of my early career was filled with examples of the kind of leader I didn't want to be.

It took getting through the layers and looking beyond the idea of the "big boss" as leader before I found a handful of examples of what I saw as true leaders. They were rarely the loudest, most confident, or most visible in the room. They also didn't necessarily look like I grew up thinking leaders should look. Real leadership was more subtle and was rarely rewarded or celebrated.

As someone who has chosen to be self-employed, I've learned the most about leadership through friends and being able to compile the best qualities they've learned from their workplaces and bosses. Namely how we can advocate for and elevate each other, not just the bottom line. In my work as a facilitator and educator, I know my biggest thrill is learning from others, not pretending to have all the answers.

What if leaders didn't have to look like they have in the past? What if the copy and paste model of how we operate got disrupted? What if we truly had other voices at the table? I think we already do.

Enter climate activist Greta Thunberg, who was fifteen when she started spending her Fridays protesting outside of Swedish parliament, or the high school students who emerged as outspoken gun-reform activists after the Parkland shooting. These "kids" have already grown wise beyond their years and show us a glimmer that there's another way.

But we can't ignore the "what if." What if we lived in a world where we didn't need to have kids step into the roles of adults? The power of youth is they show us bravery and courage. New generations aren't here to uphold old programming. They're actively fighting for a better future for themselves, and the world.

In his book *This Could Be Our Future*, Kickstarter cofounder Yancey Strickler wrote a manifesto for a more generous world, breaking down our broken system of values. He points out how the concept of financial maximization is the guiding force for much decision-making. When financial decisions reign supreme we don't consider other factors, namely humans, the environment, waste, etc.

Ben Cohen and Jerry Greenfield, who became famous for their local Vermont ice cream felt that their salaries should be five times that of the lowest-paid worker when the brand took off. While the 5:1 ratio rose over time and they eventually sold their company to Unilever, this way of thinking remains a mindset and ethos that is not common today. (Curious to learn about social justice or climate issues? Check out Benandjerrys.com or their social media accounts for a true education—likely one you didn't get in school.)

Another figure who has broken the mold of how to run a business is Yvon Chouinard, the founder of Patagonia. His ethos has always put the outdoors ahead of financial gains. Because of this (and a standout childcare program), employee retention is high. Fast-forward to 2022, when Chouinard announced that he was giving his company away. He actively wanted out of the billionaires club, opted to pay high taxes, and ensured that the earnings of his company would go to support climate efforts. This wasn't about ego. It was about another way.

Our passions and life experience can inspire us to show up in the world in different ways. Sometimes there are things we can no longer be silent about. Sometimes an issue may need our spin, our perspective or line of questioning, and our way of sharing to resonate with others. We tend to underestimate just how powerful being our full, authentic self can be.

PONDER:

What does real leadership look like to you? Write the names of folks who inspire you in the margins of this book.

PLAYGROUND! MINDMAP INSPIRING PEOPLE

Create a mindmap of people who inspire you in terms of how they lead, their values, how they operate in the world. Dig down to what it is about them that draws you to them.

Work and identity.

Many people don't know who they are without work. It's deeply rooted in our identity. Can you answer "how are you?" without talking about your job? Does your job complete you? Do you have a life outside of work? Do you measure your success by how much work you got done? If your job disappeared tomorrow, how would you react?

The challenge to unhook identity from work and productivity is real. Our ego gets wound up in it too. Productivity gives us the sense that we're accomplished—it's what we see rewarded. We can fall into workaholism as a way to feel desired, valued, and worthy.

In our societal and familial conditioning, as well as social constructs, we can internalize certain messages around work and what work looks like, sometimes overcompensating to prove ourselves, concerned with how others will perceive us, or if we'll be accepted. Society wants and expects you to fit into boxes and have life all figured out, but so much of life is an illusion. We also can place value or judgment on others because of this programming. My grad school professors often are more impressed when I can name-drop a big established brand I've worked for than by the fact that I created my business from the ground up in a different country and have built my own client list.

The question "Who are you without the doing?" is one that has stuck with me since I heard it on Jocelyn Glei's podcast *Hurry Slowly*. Our systems love and reward the doing. But what if we did less? And what if our work didn't have to define us or make us interesting?

We're a society obsessed with productivity, and then we're hard on ourselves when we're not productive. We rarely pause to reflect if our attitudes towards work may be outdated too. Oliver Burkeman's *Four Thousand Weeks: Time Management for Mortals* is a nod to the average life span. It doesn't offer tips to be more productive so much as a reframe of how we want to spend the time we do have— we can't do it all.

The challenge to unhook work from identity is heightened by technology. Especially with the increased popularity of remote work, there's even less separation. We're always reachable. We want to be liked, and we risk falling into people-pleasing tendencies to be perceived as a team player. Do we ever lose ourselves in the process?

Navigating life transitions is challenging, particularly around work because of this attachment to identity. Whether changing jobs, losing a job, working through burnout, or entering retirement, it's hard to disconnect our identity from what we've always known and been rewarded for or associated with. Few people are open about the discomfort of these life transitions and how solitary or jarring it can feel.

It's a process to unhook ourselves from what we know. The importance of override is reminding ourselves that we're fully worthy and deserving as human beings, independent of any other factors in our lives. Returning to our values as an anchor can help us come back to ourselves.

PONDER:

Explore your employment (or schooling) history alongside your relationship with productivity. How does your workplace reward certain ways of working (e.g., late nights, long hours, going above and beyond), and disapprove of others (unplugging, taking time off)? Do you fear how you would be perceived if you weren't doing the work you're doing? What really matters to you in your job? If you have kids, what do you want to model for them when it comes to work?

PLAYGROUND! VALUES

Write a list of 10–15 values that are important to you (search "values list" on the internet). Narrow down the list, and circle the 3–5 that are most essential to you. Turn it into a daily, weekly, or monthly practice to revisit your values. Regular check-ins ensure we're operating according to our own authentic self, rather than society's metrics. (Check out my Write Your Own Rules mini workshop for added support.)

The need for external validation.

As kids we were trained through validation, praise, and rewards, working for good grades or getting a gold star sticker for doing tasks. As adults, external validation doesn't work the same. Yet we still want a sense of approval, and confirmation that we're doing something "right."

We start to question ourselves, looking outside ourselves rather than trusting that the answers are within us. It can be easy to lose motivation when there are no outside factors to nudge us forward. At the same time, we may feel this strange need to prove ourselves. We crave positive reinforcement. We stop trusting ourselves along the way.

Some of the need for validation also comes from fear of rejection. We want to be chosen. Rejection—or any life curveball—may just be redirection and can hold lessons and beauty after the initial shock. Even if things don't go as planned, we're learning and evolving each step of the way.

When we do things differently from how they have always been done, there won't necessarily be immediate proof of our efforts. We must keep going. We have to trust our own way before we can lead the way that others can follow (it may take time—even decades). That's why it's essential to stay in our own lane as we build trust muscles. The best rewards likely aren't tangible, but ones you can feel on the inside in terms of what lights you up. This is true alignment.

To override successfully, it's an inside job. It's making changes from the inside out, not waiting for approval, praise, or validation. Part of the process of overriding involves releasing attachment to external factors. There is no need to prove yourself. Trust yourself. Intuition over ego. It's believing in yourself deeply, even when we can't quite see the fruits of our labors. Overriding also means not needing someone else to tell us what our next move is. It's listening to ourselves.

PONDER:
What if everything you need is already inside you?

PRACTICE:
When you find yourself needing affirmation or validation or caring what others think, talk to yourself as if you were talking to your five-year-old self. What would you tell them? How would you support them in this moment?

Inspired by Mel Robbins of *The High Five Habit*, you can also give yourself a high five in the mirror. Be your biggest cheerleader. (And stop caring what other people think.)

Dopamine of instant gratification.

We grew up being taught good things come to those who wait, yet the world has become one that struggles to see past instant gratification. If something doesn't work out on the first try or happen immediately, we can default to thinking it's not working or we're doing something wrong. Once again, we never learned about discomfort as a natural part of the growth process. We want to be good at something out of the gate, rather than embracing the awkwardness of trying something new. Fast is not always better.

Social media platforms are designed to keep us hooked and coming back infinitely. We're validated through likes and followers and external factors. The algorithm feeds us hits of dopamine designed to keep us hooked. (Societal systems and our jobs—those "perks"—do too to keep us in the matrix!) We're nudged to do things in a way that favors the system rather than our intuition. It doesn't have to be that way.

PONDER:
Where in your life do you value speed over long-term gratification? In a world of instant gratification, what if the things you truly desire just take time?

Our relationship with time.

We love giving ourselves a timeline and deadline for getting things done, yet very rarely does life stick to the timelines we assign it (if it does, it may also come at a cost). There's a lot on our plates. We can be guilty of beating ourselves up for being behind (another construct). We rarely pause to question timelines or ask if there are enough resources to set us up for success.

What if we could slow down enough to **allow things to take the time they take?**

Instead of repeating the way we've always seen things done before, we finish faster with a more impactful result when our cup is still full. Allowing ourselves time, buffer, and a cushion is intertwined with granting ourselves grace and space for life to happen.

PONDER:
What is the scariest thing about allowing yourself time? What if we could play with time in a way that opens up space rather than treat time as something scarce? What if we accepted that things likely will take longer than the timelines we assign? Deadlines are real—how might we redesign expectations?

Resistance to less vs. more.

What keeps you from doing less? Working less? Owning less? When was the last time you did less instead of more? Underdelivered instead of overdelivered? Got things done rather than perfect?

We live in a world where more is somehow seen as better, yet at the same time, everyone is overwhelmed and has limited bandwidth, functioning at or over capacity. Each thing we add to our to-do list is actually composed of dozens of invisible steps. Technology masks a lot too. We can't always see all the work we're doing or all the stuff we're accumulating.

You may find yourself spring cleaning or Marie Kondo—ing life, but how did it get to the point where there was so much stuff to begin with? Stuff isn't limited to the physical; our digital worlds are also full, and our minds are cluttered with information too. The mind may be juggling a job, life, caregiving, etc. How we haven't hit system overload before now is beyond me!

Just as busy isn't a badge of honor, more isn't either. It's a matter of discernment of what is actually necessary, and what brings us joy. We need to have time and bandwidth to take this step. What if doing less was scheduled into our calendars? (A mandatory rest period that's longer than society deems "acceptable.")

My working theory is that the less we do, the more we can achieve (not that more is the barometer of success). Few people are comfortable attempting that. What if less could give us a different kind of "more" in our life? More space, more freedom, more fulfillment, more delight.

PONDER:

What are the stories you're telling yourself that make more better? What is your relationship to physical objects?

PRACTICE:

What in your life can you let go of, both physically and digitally, or even mentally? Often in order to find other ways, we need to make literal space for ourselves. It's not all or nothing. Small steps, over time.

The speed of life.

We accept speed as the norm rather than the reality: overwhelm, distraction, and the race to be "the best." It's too much to compute. **System overload.** It's actually quite miraculous that we function at all, come to think of it. Why are we so afraid to slow down?

Speed can serve as an excellent strategy to avoid other ways. We make excuses and tell ourselves "this is how it is," or "I'll do that later, or when I retire." Yet we cannot predict the future.

Information moves so fast that our brains can feel scrambled. Technology doesn't always add ease; there's yet another invisible layer of work. It's important too to note that many roles were conceived in an era before there were a million pieces of information coming at us at all hours 24/7 (not to mention gendered roles that assumed women didn't work and took care of the home and children). We've never been so connected, yet disconnected at the same time. Support systems have never been so stressed. We're always optimizing, but at what cost?

Each task requires gear switching, which adds to the

drain. We weren't designed to move through life like this optimization-obsessed world currently operates. Life alone is a full-time job between buying groceries, keeping a home in order, paying bills, going to the doctor, chasing packages, things breaking . . . it's endless. And exhausting. Yet we can barely admit we're exhausted. We're too in it to acknowledge how we really feel. We can't look weak. We worry too much about what others think, or carry guilt for giving someone else more to do.

No one teaches us that life is also about upkeep and maintenance, nor builds in time for it. In our system override, what if we built in time for things to go wrong? What if companies built in time and space for maintenance, upkeep, and the unexpected? We need this in everyday life too.

In this whirlwind of life, we can turn to nature for a much-needed reminder. Like nature, there are seasons for flowers and harvest and other times where we need to rest and nest, or what author Katherine May refers to as "Wintering." The fallow times are essential to see the fruits of our labors.

My slowest seasons of life—a natural cocooning—are when my greatest transformations have taken place. Slowing down is letting go of the idea that we have to do it all.

PONDER:
What if slowing down was how you gained time? What if slowing down was how we flourished and thrived? (If you feel resistance to these ideas, explore that as well.)

Procrastination vs. percolation.

What if procrastinating had an upside? People around us are constantly talking about feeling lazy or behind. The messaging we absorb is around inadequacy, failure, and not doing or being enough. If we're not productive we're somehow not inherently worthy?!? This programming is not supportive. I prefer looking for **progress > productivity**.

I've come to learn that sometimes when I'm procrastinating, I'm actually working on the wrong thing. I'm doing the thing that is the distraction, rather than the thing that excites me and lights me up. The avoidance is actually trying to tell me something (another way?), but I don't want to listen, or perhaps I'm overcomplicating something.

Other times I really do just need time to think through something. Walks help a lot with this. Then when the time is right, it flows. Letting go of trying to force anything opens so many channels to possibility. Trust the process. One thing at a time and it will all get done.

PONDER:
Are you allowing yourself to work on the thing you really want to be doing, or are you focused on a distraction?

Burnout.

Too often the override feature is used to ignore our intuition and better judgment resulting in things like burnout. (The opposite of what we're seeking to override in this book.) Our goal is to be proactive, not reactive and stop it before it starts. We can't make change if we're burned out.

The pressure to keep going is real in society. "I've just got to get through X then I can breathe again." Except everything is a moving target that never ends. We constantly feel behind or like we're playing catch up.

This is only heightened by media stories celebrating what time successful people wake up in the morning and insane hours people work. Comparison trap makes us play mind-games with ourselves. It's a vicious cycle that's hard to break out of.

When has your own body given you clues to slow down? Ask anyone who has experienced burnout. They've felt it coming. They just didn't act on it.

We're excellent at making excuses and talking ourselves out of anything that will slow us down or make us feel—or look—like we're not performing our best. (The fear of what others will think.) Much of the time it's not even an external pressure but our own drive towards unrealistic expectations. Wow, we sure put a lot of pressure on ourselves.

"Everyone else is doing so much, so there must be something wrong with me" becomes a storyline that runs through our head, or a subconscious belief that "I'll look lazy or like I'm not being a team player."

It's challenging to listen to and trust ourselves when there are so few examples around us of how to be in the world where hustle, optimization, performance, and output don't reign supreme as markers of success. There are fewer visible people who seem to model or normalize any other way of moving through the world, so the copy and paste of overwork, exhaustion, and feeling disassociated from ourselves wins. Burnout becomes the norm, not the exception.

Pause and ask yourself, What behavior do I want to model for my colleagues? My team? For my kids?

The thing about burnout is that it's often our bodies that stop us more than our own initiative to believe there is another way. It often takes a serious life event or a major health diagnosis to force us to change course. Do you ever ponder what our health systems would look like if people (and systems) actually cared for themselves along the way? If we actually listened to our bodies?

We're so entrenched in the systems and dominant cultural paradigms, only in hindsight can we see things with clarity. We could have prevented things from getting so bad (or scaling into serious health issues), yet we chose not to. We chose to ignore intuition and make excuses.

Why don't we allow ourselves to be sustainable out of the gate? What pressures are put on us? What pressures are we putting on ourselves? Why is it so scary to step away?

We're all going to go through times of life where burnout is bound to happen despite our best efforts. The Nagoski sisters, authors of *Burnout*, remind us that it's necessary to complete stress cycles. You can't just run from it; you must go through the tunnel, allowing your body to work through the stress. You need to release the pressure that is building up internally. It can't be ignored.

When we experience burnout, we can also take what we learn to inform how we approach future situations. For instance, we may want to ensure we have a lighter scheduled week after a big launch or deadline. This not only gives time for our body to recover, but our mind needs rest too.

PONDER:
When have you experienced burnout? What did it feel like? What indicators did you have? What do you what to remember going forward? Does your definition of success include anything linked to your health?

On loss.

We never talk about grief. Grief can take many forms. We can find ourselves mourning so much more than loved ones lost. We can grieve friendships, pets, the life we thought we'd be living, things we thought we wanted . . .

Grief is a letting go. It's a process. It takes time—more time than we'd like. It can creep up when you least expect. It can make anniversaries or birthdays feel raw. Grief looks so different for everyone, but the couple days off work in many places is hardly time to process. "Take all the time you need" is a saying more than a reality. And as hard, sad, or scary as it may feel, the best way through grief is to face it.

My mom's initial diagnosis of ovarian cancer was one of the events that set my own reprioritization of life and ways of operating in motion in a way that felt more aligned with myself than society's vision. The night before she passed away in 2017, I got a masterclass in loss. Through tears I found myself saying, "but this is not how it happens in the movies and TV" in response to all the waiting and not knowing. We were at home with the family and the hospice nurse, and I realized no one had prepared me for this.

When reading *Final Gifts* by hospice nurses Maggie Callanan and Patricia Kelley after losing my mom, I was struck by different narratives around saying goodbye and what happens after they are gone. Noteworthy, the person grieving isn't in a place to know what they need. They're just trying to get through one day at a time. Rather than telling the grieving person "tell me what I can do to help"—which further puts the burden on them—you can suggest a way to help, such as "I'll bring you dinner tomorrow. If you're not up for company I'll leave it at your front door."

I think a lot about how much trauma runs the show (particularly the anger in the world). Much of it stems from unprocessed grief, the narratives around of showing emotions, and the fear of the unknown. Grief can be complicated depending on your relationship. Holding in and hiding from grief doesn't make it go away. What goes unprocessed gets passed down to future generations. This is why the "override" explored in this book asks us to face these uncomfortable subjects head on as part of the unblocking and healing.

PRACTICE:
Permission to see the grief. To feel it all. Let yourself be sad, be mad, be angry, cry. Release and let it out. Allow it to be a process and take time. Like all healing, it often can take longer than the timeline we give it. After my mom passed away, I wrote memories of her for 100 days as part of my healing. Find your own way to process grief.

An incomplete, unofficial list of that which is broken.

As you read through the next section, read through it with a sense of awareness. Naming and acknowledging the realities and challenges in the world around us is a crucial first step.

None of this is about you. It's about the world you were born into. You are not powerless. You can acknowledge that multiple things can be true at once—the world around us may be broken, the systems are rigged, and we can choose how we want to show up. We can acknowledge complexity and ask ourselves, what if there was another way?

Let's name what is broken in the world as a way to move forward. In no particular order (and add your own):

1. Billionaires are not taxed

2. How billionaires are celebrated

3. Contempt and prejudice against women (misogyny)

4. Hatred of others for their skin color (racism)

5. Inflation/cost of living (and cost of lunch!)

6. Defaulting men to power (patriarchy hurts men too)

7. Politicians regulating bodies (particularly of women)

8. Outdated gender roles

9. Rich people keep getting richer while those without means struggle to get by

10. White supremacy and treatment of historically under-represented communities

11. Lack of time off to process grief (bereavement)

12. Lack of resources for mental health and invisible issues

13. Treating everyone like their brain works the same way

14. The belief that everyone can fit into boxes, or that they just have one box (gender and sexuality, etc.)

15. The desire to label everything

16. Hatred towards those who love someone of the same sex

17. The cost of war (monetary and lives)

18. Lack of investment in infrastructure/public transportation (and maintenance)

19. Making decisions solely based on financial gains

20. CEO salaries vs. salaries of essential workers

21. Poor treatment of employees by billion-dollar companies

22. Who gets punished (or a pass) in prison systems

23. The length (and cost) of campaign cycles in the US

24. Cost of education (university in the US) + debt

25. Lack of family support and cost of childcare (particularly in nonsocialized countries)

26. Internalized capitalism and emphasis on productivity

27. Colonialism + lack of care for indigenous populations

28. The cost of health "care" and insurance (in the US)

29. Lack of conversation around miscarriages

30. Lack of conversation about premature birth and trauma for all involved

31. Lack of awareness of trauma responses among those who have not experienced trauma

32. Unrealistic beauty standards

33. Easier to find a cosmetic surgeon than make an appointment to get a potentially cancerous mole checked out

34. Lack of emotional education

35. Having to make healthcare decisions due to networks and fine print rather than getting the best, fastest care

36. Lack of empathy for those with chronic illness

37. Narratives (media and otherwise) that perpetuate stereotypes and limiting beliefs that keep us stuck

38. Lack of inclusion for those who are not able-bodied, have skin of a certain color, look/behave a certain way, etc.

39. Lack of representation (age, ethnicity, religion, sexuality, gender, body positivity, etc.) in many industries

40. Leaders who make decisions based on ego and out of fear (trauma response) rather than for the people

41. Limited visibility of different approaches to life

42. Closure of local, independent shops that are the heartbeat of the city to be replaced by generic big box shops

43. The Pinterest-ification of locations and decision-making to make things Instagrammable and homogenous

44. Tech bros pretending to know everything

45. Podcast bros only elevating each other

46. Inflated tech salaries vs. teacher salaries

47. Hostility towards Jews (anti-Semitism)

48. Hatred/violence towards any ethnic or religious group

49. Perpetuation of false narratives through online platforms

50. It's easier to buy a gun (US) than get a driver's license

51. Teachers have to buy their own classroom supplies

52. GoFundMe fundraisers to pay for medical bills (US)

53. Social media algorithms

54. Doctors are supposed to help us be healthy yet work the most insane workdays (same in med school)

55. Lack of wheelchair accessibility in many places

56. Association of having things/stuff with happiness

57. Medical gaslighting (not believing patients)

58. Underpaid + poor conditions for garment workers

59. Lack of protection in cases of domestic, child abuse

60. Inadequate medical research/testing on women

61. Extremism of so many varieties

62. Consumer culture as sign of overall health of economy

63. Discrimination for age, gender, skin color, religion, etc.

64. Toxic masculinity, which perpetuates male dominance

65. Toxic positivity (which negates actual emotions)

66. Money + influence to control outcomes in their favor

67. Abuse/harm towards others, and innocent children

68. Mental/physical/emotional loads caregivers carry

69. Dismissal of lived experience in knowledge and decision-making

70. Stereotype that men don't do therapy

71. Hiring bias (particularly around age, race, sexuality)

72. Productivity and growth-obsessed culture

73. Megachurches that don't pay taxes

74. Greenwashing (pretending to be eco-friendly)

75. The way women are pitted against each other by the media as competition

76. Not listening to or believing women; defaulting to men as experts; only citing men in studies/books

77. Thinking we have to act a certain way to be loved

78.

79.

80.

81.

82.

83.

84.

85.

86.

87.

88.

89.

90.

91.

92.

93.

94.

95.

96.

97.

98.

99. *Keep going!!!*

Banana map what's broken.

Life is heavy. Life is hard. Sometimes we need a break. And sometimes we need a dose of humor, and to invite in a bit of lightness. Internalizing everything that is broken doesn't do anything to move us forward. We must get outside of ourselves and understand the world we live in.

There aren't many books that instruct you to map on a banana, but this isn't any book. This step is going to help prime you to take action in Part 3. To move forward we first must name and acknowledge realities.

Little did you know that bananas have transformative properties when you map on them. Bananas don't last forever, and you can leave any perfectionist tendencies behind. I sense some eyes rolling already, so this is your invitation to lighten up, be aware of your judgments, and stay open to trying something new.

First, you will need a banana (ideally yellow), and a ballpoint pen for maximum pleasure and enjoyment. Set a timer for five minutes. Your prompt for this exercise is to map out all the ways "everything is broken"—in other words, explore the ways that the world you live in is not the world you imagined growing up. Without overthinking it, start drawing on the banana. See what happens . . .

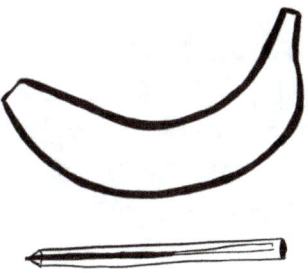

You can map out what feels broken on a personal level, or consider the world level. Remember to focus on the context of the world we live in. Doodle, draw, use words, add lines or arrows. What connections can you make that you may not have seen before?

If you don't have a banana, anything with a peel can work. Ideally use something that you typically don't write on (no paper), 3-D, and perishable if possible. We don't want to be precious with this exercise. Head to the recycling bin as another option. If we're going to override, we need to learn to get creative and get out of our comfort zones.

Don't worry, there's no grade at the end. There's no right or wrong way. Journal about the wisdom your banana revealed. It's one way to start the dialogue of change with others in your life.

Bananas don't last forever. Take a picture or video and tag @pretavoyager + #overridebananamap.

Space for reflection.

How much time do you allow for reflection in life? Let this page be a reminder to build it in. Despite sounding counterintuitive, taking time and prioritizing yourself opens up more space and time. We need moments to process.

PART 2:
An empowered mind

Engage override by shifting your mindset to open possibilities.

"To be truly visionary we have to root our imagination in our concrete reality while simultaneously imagining possibilities beyond that reality."

—BELL HOOKS, FEMINISM IS FOR EVERYBODY: PASSIONATE POLITICS

What if there was another way?

NOTES TO SELF:

What if . . . ?

"What if" is a question that can go a couple ways. It can send us into a dark fear spiral or it can open up other ways forward and invite in creative possibilities. We're interested in the "What if" line of questioning that shifts our perspective to one that's opening and curiosity-led.

The way you approach a challenge can shape an outcome, so our framing of questions or understanding of the problem is key if we want to override effectively. We don't want to limit ourselves before we even get started.

Asking "What if there was another way?" helps get us unstuck and out of repeated patterns because it invites us to move beyond a fixed way of doing things and binary thinking. It invites a way of thinking that doesn't have to rely solely on our logical or rational brain. We can expand our field of vision, acknowledging that there are possibilities out there that we have not yet considered.

PRACTICE:
Ask WHAT IF and come up with as many crazy ideas as you can. (They don't have to be good or make sense.)

Embrace the beginner's mind.

Zen Buddhist Sunryu Suzuki describes the beginner's mind by saying, "in the expert's mind there are few possibilities, but in the beginner's there are many."

There's a benefit in not knowing too much at times. Knowledge can get in our way. When we embrace the beginner's mind it further supports the question "What if there was another way?" We stay open to possibilities before closing off alternatives we may not have considered out of the gate. We get to figure things out as we go. We can imagine alternate outcomes.

When we stay open to possibilities beyond what is obvious, we can challenge assumptions. Only then can we start to override the same excuses and crutches that keep us stuck in autopilot. Take a deep breath and embrace the beginner's mind. Stay open to trying something new, and being bad at it.

PRACTICE:
When faced with a dilemma, invite yourself to think like a beginner and remove any initial limitations. Imagine a scenario from different lenses. How would a four-year-old approach this situation, or your ninety-year-old relative?

Ask more questions.

As children we're full of wonder and ask questions all the time. As adults we can get lost in the swirl of life and forget to pause to ask questions.

The "5 Whys" is a simple tool I've seen used across industries from UX design to therapy in order to get away from the obvious and gain a better understanding of what's really going on. It starts with asking a question, listening to the response, and then asking why (or another related or clarifying question), then repeat. Asking why five times helps us go beyond autopilot programming and start to understand a situation or problem at a deeper level and the ways issues or ideas are interconnected. We're trying to get away from default responses and people responding the way they think the other person wants them to.

Using open-ended questions rather than questions that have a yes/no response will get us richer results. Questions can also be framed as genuine curiosity, such as "Tell me more," or clarifying questions such as "What did you mean by . . . ?"

Seemingly awkward silences are actually golden moments when the responder can share more information that likely wouldn't have emerged otherwise. Allow people time to answer before jumping in to fill the space.

Don't be afraid to admit you don't understand something. "I know we've moved on to something else, but could you go back to [the thing you were talking about]. I was hoping you could clarify what X means/refers to." Even if you do understand, it's a way to ensure the audience is on the same page.

What we think is the problem at hand is rarely the actual issue or root cause. While society rewards having answers and values being right, more often than not there's more value in asking questions than finding solutions. In order to move past assumptions and embrace curiosity, we must practice getting comfortable not always having answers and trusting that by asking more questions we'll figure things out as we go.

PRACTICE:
Practice the 5 Whys with a friend. With each answer, keep asking why, get curious, and go beyond the surface.

Listen. Really listen.

The ability to listen is one of the most underappreciated qualities in others, and something we are not actually taught to do. In a world that fights for our attention and rewards multitasking over being present, we move too fast to truly listen and wake up.

Just because we hear something doesn't mean we fully have listened or absorbed what the other person was saying. We're all guilty of checking out and getting lost in our own thoughts, or trying to figure out what we're going to say next rather than listening to another point of view.

When working with teams, one of my favorite workshop activities is "blindfolded storytelling," where I literally have blindfolds for participants. One person tells a story—typically the prompt is something like "Tell a story about a meaningful moment in your life"—and the others listen.

It's an interesting experience for both the speaker and for the listeners that safely takes both sides out of their comfort zone in an unexpected way. It immediately invites in awkwardness and discomfort—especially when I tell listeners they're not allowed to speak or make sounds.

Suddenly participants become hyperaware of the power of listening, and also the need for connection and desire to know that others are listening when you're the one speaking. It quickly becomes clear that sometimes we tend to want to speak before we've actually listened. We're all too eager to have answers, find the solution, and fix the problem so we can move on.

Sometimes engaging override means not doing anything other than listening. A simple "that's so hard" or "I'm so proud of you" when someone tells us about something challenging they're going through is enough. It's an acknowledgment that you are listening. Humans desire to be heard and witnessed.

And while we're on the subject of listening, don't forget to listen to yourself.

PRACTICE:
Focus on listening. Have a blindfolded (or eyes closed) conversation with a friend, and pay attention to what it feels like. Ask them to tell you a story they haven't told you before. It may feel a bit awkward at first, but allow it to be an experiment. Switch roles and repeat.

Logic + intuition.

How are the ideas in this book landing in your body for you?

It's hard to press override when school trains us to only value our logical, rational brain. But there is room—and value—for following our head and our heart (and our gut).

Intuition is too often ignored. You know when something feels off. Often we ignore these clues in our body and in our being. Intuition is also a wonderful indicator light for when something is going right. You know when something lights you up—it's that full-body YES!

Intuition is called many things: inner knowing (Glennon Doyle), your north star (Martha Beck), life force (Phil Stutz), trusting your vibes (Sonia Choquette), vibrating high (Lalah Delia), listening to an itch (Rob Bell), trusting whispers (Alex Elle), getting quiet (Oprah), responding to a ping, hit, or download (Lacy Phillips), and trusting your gut.

Intuition is often subtle. There won't always be words to accompany a feeling or sensation. Intuition can't always be explained. It even can be a crazy idea that society (or friends or family) may want to talk us out of. It may not even make sense to you at the time. Intuition does not need justification—for ourselves, or for others. Intuition needs trust.

Rather than only thinking your way through this book, you're also invited to feel your way through. Pay attention to your body. When does it feel heavy? Avoidant? Resistant? Where are your wheels spinning? Are you trying to defend or justify something? (When control or fear lead the way, dig into these areas. These are golden clues worth exploring deeper.) What is your intuition trying to tell you?

PRACTICE:
Next time you need to make a big decision, get quiet before asking others. Trust yourself. Don't force an answer. Unplug. Journal. Go for a walk. Check with your gut.

PONDER:
What if you did the thing that's been screaming at you to do it, without attachment to outcome? What if you knew you tried even if you "failed"? What's the worst that could happen?

Mind-body connection.

I'm always on the hunt for when something feels right. I look for the shimmy or when my body does a little "happy dance." I feel light and lit up inside. It clicks. Laughter with tears of joy and goose bumps are other good indicators. I even feel it in my body when I hear someone else telling their own truth.

When our bodies are tense and stuck, we're naturally going to limit our possibilities. We've blocked ourselves from seeing a way to other options. Tension in the body is a perfect warning bell to alert us that something isn't working.

In Gabor Maté's *The Myth of Normal,* he explores the mind-body connection from a scientific/medical perspective and how medical treatment rarely takes the emotional or mental side of health into account. More often than not there is a connection between ailments and something deeper. Everything is connected. What would be possible if we started to connect the dots between different pieces of our being?

PRACTICE:
Tune in to your body as a barometer for decision-making.

We are all mirrors.

The world provides many opportunities for us to learn about ourselves. This could be anything from an interaction that makes us self-reflect to encountering someone who helps show us what's possible (or perhaps showing what we don't want). Mirrors can show up in different ways.

We may find ourselves giving advice to a friend that's actually the advice we need to be listening to ourselves (I call these "mirror moments"). Or maybe there's a message or theme that keeps coming up, like a book or a resource, that's worth paying attention to.

Mirrors can help reflect back to us what's really going on at a subconscious level. Pay attention to situations where you feel triggered, have a visceral reaction, or feel judgment, envy, or jealousy. You may not want what someone else has in the same way or form, but with time I've come to see mirrors hold clues to what I do desire.

PRACTICE:
Look for mirrors in your own life and ask yourself, "What can I learn from this situation?" or "What is this trying to teach/show me?"

How we respond.

So many insecurities in life come from comments other people make to us or messages we pick up around us that we absorb as true. Even questions others ask can feel personal and wounding in how we perceive them.

A bad review, negative feedback, a breakup, or getting fired can make us feel like we're a failure, when most of the time it's not about us. If we view these moments as mirrors, they often they say more about the other person than us. It feels like it's about us, but it's not.

It's normal to feel disappointed, frustrated, or upset in life. Feel what you feel, and also know it's not personal. If something gets under our skin, there's something bigger being reflected back at us to work through. How we respond—charged/heated vs. neutral—can be an indicator when there's more to explore. We can't go through life without disappointments, but we can choose how we respond.

PONDER:
Journal about a situation in your own life that felt triggering at the time. Reflect on what you learned from it and what you want to remember going forward.

The story I'm telling myself . . .

Brené Brown invites the line of questioning that starts, "The story I'm telling myself is . . ." These are stories that feel so true to us, whether they're about us or someone else. I'm the first person to admit I spiral about imagined or projected stories rather than a known reality.

While there may be some truth in these statements we tell ourselves, more often than not they're mind games. It's important to get curious to see if there's more to the story. These stories that don't serve us can become self-limiting beliefs that start running the show, and blocking possibilities. Only when we are able to spot them can we rewrite and override them with a story that actually supports us.

Naming what's going on by saying "The story I'm telling myself is [they don't like me, I did a bad job, I'm not cool enough . . .]" can be very freeing. You're allowed to feel, but also release and reframe what's not supportive.

PRACTICE:
The story I'm telling myself is [insert story here], AND I WONDER IF there's something else going on? Is this really true?

Reframe the way you see things.

With my own clients, I have a "limiting belief alarm" where I wave my arms to get their attention and make them pause before continuing so they can hear themselves. My flailing helps lighten the mood.

It happens when I hear a statement that they make out loud, unaware of the limits they're putting on themselves through the words they're using. The way they speak has become an invisible hurdle keeping them from getting where they want to go. *Are you sure you have to do that before you start? Why do you believe "this or that" are your only options?*

Let this be your invitation to shift and expand how you've always viewed the world. You get to choose how you frame the experience and empower yourself to look at it through a lens and a mindset that are supportive of the world you want to live in.

While we all can easily get sucked into how things have always been done or a negative mindset given all the challenges in the world, that doesn't mean it's the only way, or that it has to stay that way forever. You can turn your day/week/month/year around through shifting how you frame these stories.

Once we have become aware of the limiting beliefs or outdated stories we've come to accept as truth, we can reframe them to something more supportive, expansive, and empowered. Notice in your body—there's a shift when you are able to reframe a statement. Go for lightness and ease.

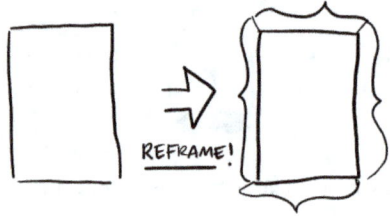

If we're stuck believing the world is a certain way, it's going to continue to be that way. Changing how we talk about it—and about ourselves—is necessary to help shape a different outcome. We're shifting our perspective to one where anything is possible.

PRACTICE:
Pay attention to where your attention goes and what gets repeated and reinforced in your brain. Write down any limiting or negative beliefs you have. Cross them out and rewrite them in a way that opens possibilities.

PLAYGROUND!

Rewrite old stories that need a refresh. The pages that follow will provide more examples too.

OLD STORY:

REFRAME:

OLD STORY:

REFRAME:

OLD STORY:

REFRAME:

OLD STORY:

REFRAME:

OLD STORY:

REFRAME:

Watch your words. Flip the script.

In a Deep Writing workshop I took with psychotherapist and creative coach Eric Maisel, he suggested the question "Is this a thought that serves me?" It was one of the first times I became aware of how my thoughts were limiting my potential.

The words and language we use can shape our experience of the world. We often don't realize the power they have over the actions we take—or don't take. We say something as if to make it true. Subtle shifts like saying you're facing a challenge rather than you have a problem can change how you show up for yourself.

The words we use can not only deeply impact our own experiences but also affect our interactions with others. We can get blocked around a particular subject because of the word choice of a speaker/writer that may not resonate with us. In those cases, finding an alternative term or phrase to communicate the same message that does resonate with us can shift everything. For instance, battle language doesn't resonate with everyone who has cancer.

A key way to override old thought patterns is through

language. Limiting beliefs become reinforced through the words we use, even through the seemingly simplest of statements. When we find ourselves saying "I can't," "I don't," or "I'm bad at" over and over, it can become self-fulfilling (or rather, self-sabotaging). When we take these statements as truth we inadvertently reinforce them through our actions (or inaction).

When we use language where we believe in ourselves and a better future, we can see how the world opens up to us. A simple shift in the language we use can help inform possible steps we can take. "I'm working on," "I'm practicing," and "I am" are good openers—there's a sense of progress, and taking tangible steps towards a desired outcome, not just thinking about it.

Turn the limitation on its head and let it be an experiment, as if to say, "let me see for myself." Practice owning a different identity. *I am a writer. I am an artist. I am a cook. I am changing the world.* How would you show up differently with this mindset? (Look for action strategy "Storyboard your story" in Part 3.)

PRACTICE:

Flip negative scripts. Add "I'm working on," "I'm practicing," or "I am" to the start of any limiting beliefs that you've encountered. It may take a few revisions to get to a statement you feel that you can get behind.

Reprogram your brain.

Our mindset is important because we have the power to reprogram our brain resulting in more aligned actions. Our brains have neural pathways that are like a blueprint of our belief systems. We are shaped by our experiences in life, and those experiences and ways of thinking get "carved" and etched into our brain. Just like it's easier to hike on an existing path through the woods, it's easier to follow the existing paths rather than paving a new direction. There are times we want to take a different route.

The first time you take a new route there may be more resistance, or obstacles. That doesn't mean it's not the better route ultimately; it just may take a few times through to really clear and pave the new path. The same thing is happening when we're rewriting old stories—we're rewiring our brain in favor of new, more supportive beliefs.

Neuroscientist Dr. Tara Swart was my gateway into thinking differently. She bridges neuroscience with her background in psychiatry and interest in spirituality as an advisor to To Be Magnetic program and *Expanded* podcast, where she provided a new pathway for my brain to believe in what's possible.

Scientifically this ability to change pathways in our brain is referred to as neuroplasticity, as in our brain is malleable. The science behind "neurons that fire together wire together" helps explain how we're able to update the way we think about things. Neuroscientist Dr. David Eagleman prefers to talk about these pathways as livewired, meaning we can make new connections at any time, rather than pathways changing shape and staying that way forever.

Know this is great news for you (and all of us!). It's yet another reminder that there's room for change and possibility—this time from the inside out. Our brains are not fixed for life, meaning our belief systems can grow. This starts with our belief in ourselves! Changing our thought patterns can help us get out of our own way. Our brains are proof that the world in front of us is limitless!

The goal is to reprogram old stories with supportive ones than can move us as individuals—and a world—forward. There may be *aha!* moments, but it will take repetition, reinforcement, and time for these reframes to take hold. Reprogramming happens over time through aligned action. Revisiting this book often is one way to help reinforce these new thought patterns and neural pathways.

PRACTICE:
Choose one of your new reframes or empowered beliefs. Rewrite the phrase over and over, filling a page every day until you fully believe it. (Look for action strategy "Tap into your mind" in Part 3 too.)

Fixed vs. growth mindset.

It can be easy to go through life thinking you, or the world, are a certain way because that's the only way that you know. This is a very limited vision. It's a fixed mindset.

In her book *Mindset: Changing the Way You Think to Fulfill Your Potential*, Dr. Carol S. Dweck explores fixed mindset (closed) vs. growth mindset (open). A fixed mind doesn't allow for change, as if to say this is how it's always been done and therefore is how it will be for eternity. Meanwhile, a growth mindset allows for agency and openness, which is where we can see and do things differently. Change is possible with a growth mindset.

According to Dweck, "In the fixed mindset, everything is about the outcome. If you fail—or if you're not the best—it's all been wasted. The growth mindset allows people to value what they're doing regardless of the outcome. They're tackling problems, charting new courses, working on important issues. Maybe they haven't found the cure for cancer, but the search was deeply meaningful."

Knowing that our brains and pathways are malleable is what allows us to embrace this spirit of growth and development. See how these reframes can change how you show up to a situation:

Fixed: I could never do X. = *results in not doing anything*
Growth: I won't know unless I try. = *inspires action*

Fixed: It's not worth doing unless [excuse]. = *inaction*
Growth: If it doesn't work out I'll learn from the process. = *try*

Fixed: This is how I am. = *no room for growth*
Growth: I know this about myself AND I know that I can do anything I put my mind to. = *two things can be true*

Fixed: I have to catch up / do XYZ before I start. = *excuse*
Growth: I can start where I am, imperfectly. = *make effort*

PRACTICE:

While we're not here to judge or compare ourselves to others, it's often easier to see limiting beliefs and blocks in others rather than ourselves (remember, they can be mirrors). You can keep it to yourself, but start listening for comments others make that feel limited, closed, or fixed.

Use what you observe in others to catch where you may be more fixed in your mindset than you originally thought. This gives us clues to where we may be limiting our potential. Ask yourself what would the same scenario look like from a growth mindset or more empowered reframe? Capture it on the reframe playground page.

Scarcity vs. abundance.

The spirit of abundance contains multitudes, openness, possibility, room for all. Scarcity is linked to lack, urgency, never being enough, fear, or imposed limits.

A scarcity mindset limits possibilities before we even start and can keep us playing small or "safe." We talk ourselves out of things and tell ourselves we're not enough (good enough, smart enough, interesting enough, creative enough, educated enough, pretty enough). It tells us we can't do something because someone else is already doing it, doing it better than we can, or there's no room for us. Scarcity is urgency: *Only two left! BUY NOW or lose out!!!* There's fear and insecurity linked to scarcity.

Abundance mindset is a view without limits, which allows us see and stay open to possibilities. An abundance mindset is "Shine Theory" in action. Shine Theory is a term coined by Aminatou Sow and Ann Friedman that celebrates a mindset where there's room for everyone to succeed: "I don't shine if you don't shine." It makes you think about how you can help elevate others while also working towards your own goals.

It's amazing how a simple shift can open up possibilities.

Scarcity: I can't do X because [person] already is.
Abundance: There's room for everyone. Everyone gets to bring their own secret sauce to make it their own.

Scarcity: I have to do X because it's how I make money.
Abundance: I wonder what other ways I could make money...

Scarcity: I'm not good enough to [do the thing].
Abundance: I'll get better if I take small steps.

Scarcity: There are no jobs out there.
Abundance: There are opportunities out there. I haven't found the right job for me YET.

Scarcity: It's too late. I'm [fill in the excuse].
Abundance: Despite what society tells me, it's never too late. I can inspire others through my journey.

Scarcity: That training is too expensive and won't help me.
Abundance: Investing in myself is worth the return.

If you look closer you can see how an abundance mindset allows for more curiosity and action than a scarcity mindset.

PONDER:
Reflect on times in your life when you have acted out of a scarcity mindset vs. an abundance mindset. Where are areas in your life where you have more scarcity? Abundance?

It's all a spectrum.

Life is not either/or, black or white, this or that, all or nothing, go big or go home, binary. There are a multitude of possibilities in the middle, and often tension between them. Too often we get stuck in one way of thinking.

Considering ideas as a spectrum can help us see the range of perspectives rather than a definitive outcome. In *The Culture Map*, Erin Meyer maps different cultures on a spectrum to explore how people/cultures communicate in relationship to one another, which allows for understanding.

I like to think of spectrums like someone playing the accordion. The instrument closed is compact and unsuspecting. As the musician plays, they open their arms and move it in different ways, playing keys with different notes. When expanding beliefs, imagine your hands close together. Open them outward as you open an alternative solution to the obvious, giving sound to possibilities.

PRACTICE:

Examine your ideas across a spectrum. Create your own categories as needed. Ask yourself questions and plot different points to examine where your ideas fall. For instance, do you feel worthy of that job or raise? If it's not where you want it to be, there's your sign it's an area you can work on.

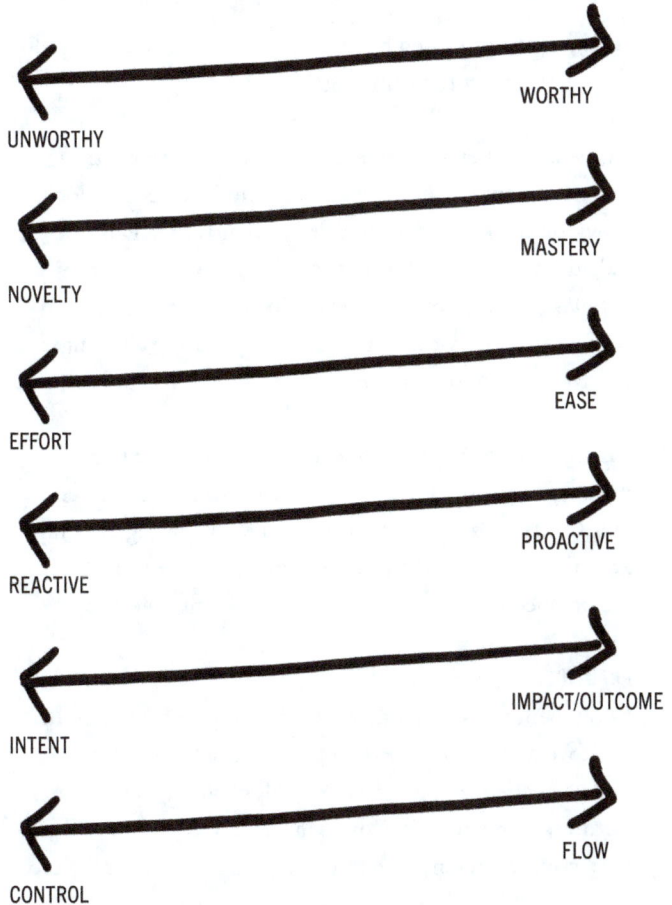

WORTHY

UNWORTHY

MASTERY

NOVELTY

EASE

EFFORT

PROACTIVE

REACTIVE

IMPACT/OUTCOME

INTENT

FLOW

CONTROL

Zoom in. Zoom out.

Looking at something from multiple perspectives can help free us from limited thinking.

Think about being on the ground and seeing something, but what happens if you were to go up in a tree and look down on it from above? Similarly, what we see with the naked eye is different from that of a microscope, magnifying glass, or telescope. Zooming in and zooming out can be helpful as we work through understanding challenges. Micro and macro. Examine details and big-picture context.

The concept of "swarming" originally links back to a military term that looks at a problem from many different directions at the same time. In fact, zooming out and zooming in was how this book came to be. I needed multiple perspectives to understand how it all fit together.

PRACTICE:
Often being able to name what's actually going on can help us move forward rather than having to solve anything. Take a challenge you're facing and look at any immediate hurdles, then zoom out for a global view. Sometimes drawing a visual representation can give you a new perspective too.

Creative constraints.

Limitations and constraints can be frustrating and annoying. Or we can reframe them to be freeing and generative. Constraints help us know what we can and can't do. They become a playground where we can open up creativity through narrowing the zone of focus, often resulting in more imaginative solutions.

There's a good chance you've told yourself, "If I just had more time, I could do XYZ." We think we need more time, space, money, you name it. Then when we have the time, we feel paralyzed (or burned out). There's always an excuse.

What if constraints actually helped us override how we thought things needed to be done and allowed us to be more creative? I know I wouldn't be doing the work I'm doing today had it not been for the "creative constraints" of French bureaucracy, which made me rethink my approach. I make people map on bananas as my own creative constraint.

PRACTICE:
Impose a constraint—time, color, materials, space, cost, deadline, etc.—on something you're working on and see what happens.

Alternative narratives.

Going through life thinking things have to be done a certain way only perpetuates the status quo. "Alternative narratives" is a term I've adopted to serve as a lens through which we can see other ways of doing things that's outside of the mainstream. It's changing the "popular" narrative to a more supportive one. (And no, alternative narratives have nothing to do with "alternative facts" or "fake news.")

"Alternative" doesn't have to be wild, crazy, or out there (but it can be). Alternative narratives are another simple way we can innovate. Think: disrupter. This applies not just to products and services but also to ways of working or how we move through the world or approach challenges.

Gabrielle Blair (aka @designmom), a Mormon mom of six, made a splash when her Twitter thread about abortions went viral. She expanded it into a book, *Ejaculate Responsibly*, with 28 short essays arguing that men are 100% responsible for unwanted pregnancies. She used her unique voice to turn a heated topic upside down and make any reader think.

Can't do work remotely? Throw in a worldwide pandemic

and see what happens from there! Telling yourself the story that you don't like something? Get thrown into a situation where you have to try it, and discover it's actually pretty great. (I thought I'd hate coaching online, but it turns out I LOVE how I can bring together international cohorts.) Who says a five-day, 40-hour workweek is the only way? Why not 15 hours over four days? Or less?

Someone tells you you can't do something because they've never seen it done before? Show them there's another way!

Seeing is believing. When we see scenarios successfully lived out by others, we can start to believe there may be other approaches and possibilities for ourselves. We can shift the narrative.

PRACTICE:

Start a collection of voices and approaches that resonate with you. Keep a list of examples of inspiring people, places, and organizations who are taking different approaches to how things are typically done. (Lacy Phillips of To Be Magnetic calls these "expanders"; I've come to see them as guides.)

This could be as simple as a note on your phone or a secret board on Pinterest. This list can help show you another way is possible. Revisit it regularly as a reminder that you don't have to do things like everyone else. Pull your inspiration from different domains and unlikely places as you create your own recipe for being in the world.

Everything is energy.

Years ago during a follow-up ER visit in Paris, I received the best medical advice of my life: cut the toxic people out of your life. It came from an older female doctor questioning my diagnosis (my tongue had mysteriously turned white). She started inquiring about how stressed I was. I didn't think I was stressed—at least not compared to others. She kept asking questions, and after I told her about my landlord (who was nice enough on the surface, but ultimately emotionally abusive), she told me to cut the toxic people out of my life. I'm grateful for her words. It made me realize how subtle some energies can be.

Just because a situation isn't the worst ever, that doesn't mean it's supporting you. For me it meant finding a new apartment, which was a long-overdue step I needed in life from my tiny (16 m²/172 ft²) seventh-floor Paris walk-up. (I think my tongue wanted me to uplevel and make space for bigger things in life.)

Subconsciously a situation may be affecting you, but it takes a conscious shift to change the energy or the situation you're in. Of course, you don't always have the luxury to cut everyone who is energetically toxic to you out of your life, but you can work on creating boundaries or reconsider the contexts in which you interact with them.

Energy affects how we show up in the world and view a situation. Resentment, judgment, anger, and anxiety are not neutral. You can feel in your body when these elements come into play. It's not the good kind of energy we want.

You know what it feels like when you're around people who bring you energy. They make you feel alive, you lose track of time, it feels fun and easy (the energy fountains). On the flip side, there are people who can drain you with their negative energy, constant know-everything/fixer advice, and general bad vibes (the energy drains or vampires).

Paying attention to the energy you bring into a situation is equally important and may influence the interaction. If you go into a meeting in a bad mood or distracted, you're bringing that energy with you. Consider how you can hit a quick reset or shake things off (literally shake your body or go for a walk) to clear the energy.

PRACTICE:

How we structure our days can affect our energy and flow. Map out your energy. Look at people, types of events/ activities, places, and time of day through the lens of what brings and takes your energy. Experiment with new boundaries and moving pieces around (changing one thing at a time), to see how it affects your energy.

Begin anywhere.
Start where you are.

One of the biggest blocks that I've seen in clients (or potential clients) is this mythical idea that they're supposed to have a grand plan figured out before being able to start. They quickly become frozen in time, adding to the overwhelm. The spiral of "being responsible," the "should dos," the "it's too lates," and guilt takes over.

You know more than you think. Chances are you know what you don't want. The way through is starting. We do this by putting one foot in front of the other. The real insights come from taking action, not thinking about what might happen or what we want to happen. Action unlocks clarity rooted in reality, rather than hypotheticals, to carry us forward. Start before you're ready.

Small steps over time lead to giant leaps. You're moving the needle forward. Face the fear and do it anyway. It's OK if you figure things out as you go. Start anywhere. Just start.

PONDER:
How would you like to FEEL today? What small action can you take to achieve that?

Action breeds confidence.

Taking action is essential to override. You don't make real progress by only thinking about it. The more action you take, the more you'll build confidence. Action breaks the cycle of avoidance, overwhelm, and fear, putting another way into motion. It's much easier for an object in motion to stay in motion.

Too often we can sit around waiting to take action because we want to feel confident in order to take the first step. This too can keep us stuck. It's scary to do something before we feel "ready," and we're not trained to operate this way.

We can tell ourselves things like "Once I [have/feel X] I will [do Y]." It's as if having the thing or reaching the milestone will finally make us feel worthy and deserving of what we want in life. Life doesn't work like this, though.

When we take action, we build trust muscles over time so we can keep going no matter what life throws our way.

PONDER:
Ask yourself, What is one small (tiny!) action I can take today towards the thing I desire?

PLAYGROUND!

What empowered mindset, reframe, or reminder would you plaster on a billboard to see every day? Write it below (on the page or on a sticky note). Consider making this reminder the background of your phone, or put a note on your bathroom mirror or by your desk to see daily to etch it into your brain. Make sure your actions reflect this mindset to truly embody it.

PART 3: Action to override

Small steps in the right direction add up over time. Action is how change happens. Taking action is how we override.

"I worry about what I have control over. I don't worry about what I have no control over."

—MY MOM

What if there was another way?

NOTES TO SELF:

Look how far you've come!

It's time for a check-in to see and celebrate just how far you've come and all the insights you've unlocked! Things are in motion now. Here's a reminder of where we've been and where we're going as we reinforce new pathways.

Part 1: A world of illusions invited you to consider why the world is the way it is. You may have discovered blocks or old stories you want to let go of in your own life, or had new clarity in how you want to work towards overriding systemic challenges. What is key is that you can see, name, and acknowledge what's at play.

Part 2: An empowered mind helped us see how the way we view the world may be affecting the actions we do—or don't—take. When we reframe old stories and shift our mindset, we can open possibilities, hope, and healing.

Part 3: Action to override is where you take action to reinforce your new, empowered beliefs. Imperfect action is still action. Try out the tools and strategies. Have fun and put your own spin on things—what works for me won't necessarily work for you. Overriding is also play as we explore, change the channel, practice, and support ourselves.

NOTE YOUR FAVORITES + ADD YOUR OWN TOOLS OR STRATEGIES:

EXPLORE

The world is your playground.

Follow your curiosity.

Part of disrupting the status quo comes from taking a detour from our norms and routines and following our curiosity. Ask yourself, "What am I curious about today?"

One curiosity may lead to another. Go down the rabbit hole. Don't be surprised if different seasons of life or what's going on in the world may take you in directions you never expected. Don't be afraid to try that thing that you've always been wanting to do. Prioritize what excites you. What's the most random thing that you can think of?

TRY THIS:

Read a book, listen to a podcast, visit a new location, or try a new skill that piques your interest about a subject you've never explored before. Follow your inner desires. (There are amazing resources in the back of this book—go where you feel pulled.)

Journaling.

Journaling is an incredibly simple and accessible tool to help us process information, feelings, frustrations. It's also why questions and prompts are integrated into this book.

Go for pen and paper. I use cheap notebooks so I'm not too precious about journaling (and as soon as an idea pops into my head, I capture it in the notes app of my phone to explore later). Journaling is my fast track to clarity, whether it's brainstorming and writing through ideas and intentions for workshop planning or exploring something I want to bring to therapy. Julia Cameron, who popularized the concept of "morning pages" in her book *The Artist's Way*, writes three longhand stream-of-consciousness pages every morning to "unclog the gutter." Elizabeth Gilbert of *Big Magic* has a practice where she starts, "Dear love, what do I need to know today?" and the pen answers.

Your journal is not for anyone other than yourself, so experiment and remove judgment. Some people never reread their journals; others do as a way to see growth.

TRY THIS:
Fill a journal page with ramblings from your brain.

Go for a wander.

Our bodies were designed to move, not sit in chairs all day staring at screens. Movement is how we feel alive. One of the simplest (and most affordable) ways to do this is to go for a walk. Even going for a walk around the block can have quick benefits.

Movement not only helps move the energy through us, we're also wiring new pathways in our brain. When we physically move our bodies, we're able to get outside of ourselves, out of our heads, and into our bodies.

Just like Steve Jobs, my favorite meetings are done while walking, or I love a "walk & talk" where I call a friend on the phone and we both go for a walk.

Street Wisdom is a wanderful way to open yourself to the world around you. It involves a series of tune-ups that encourage us to pay attention to what we notice (and what we don't), to slooowwwwww waaaayyyyyyyy downnnnnn, and to find the beauty in everything before going out on a "quest" where we take a question out into the world. (The prompts are free to listen to online on Spotify.)

During a Street Wisdom wander, I first noticed a moving truck with the tagline "moving your way." It not only struck me, but I've spotted one of those moving trucks nearly daily for over three years now. I appreciate the reminder to do things "my way," and it's almost a game now; it makes me smile every time I see one. (I also happened to wander into Keanu Reeves filming *John Wick 4* in my neighborhood in Paris on that same wander.)

There is also power in going for a walk with nothing in our ears to take in the world around us. For over a decade Libby DeLana has gone for a walk, which she captures through *This Morning Walk*. She's the first to celebrate the transformative power of walking and the clarity and insights the simple act reveals.

Think of walking as a highly refined yet underutilized processing tool. It sounds so simple that we don't do it. Sometimes a wander is just what we need to override the old stories and start to see new possibilities we've never considered.

TRY THIS:
Go for a walk the next time you start to feel stuck or frustrated and see what happens. Better yet, integrate it as part of your daily practice that becomes a priority.

Head to nature.

Green spaces have long been shown to hold psychological benefits and help us regulate our nervous system as a way to be grounded. Green space can be one of the fastest ways to recharge your batteries. Green spaces are a refuge and escape from the everyday.

You may be lucky enough to have a yard or green space nearby. Those of us in cities may need to head to a park or even go further afield to find actual nature.

Nature is naturally soothing. "Forest bathing" is a concept that was made popular in Japan in the 1980s as a form of "ecotherapy," acknowledging the benefits of the natural world to our health. There's no actual bathing but rather basking in a green, natural environment.

TRY THIS:
Go forth and find a green space.

Get outside of your everyday.

We need to get out to break out of autopilot. Travel has been one of the most expansive tools in my toolkit. Travel allows us to experience firsthand that there's another way, whether it's visiting another neighborhood or community or traveling to another country.

You need not go far for travel to find insights. When I started my travel blog, *Prêt à Voyager* (translation: ready to travel), in 2007, I adopted the mantra "travel is not about where you go but how you see the world." My dad always said politicians should take the train. Unlike highways, trains take you through places where people actually live.

In *The Artist's Way*, Julia Cameron suggests weekly "artist dates" to experience something new. Intentionally get yourself out and into the world and look at life through fresh eyes. Journalist Rob Walker would call this the "Art of Noticing."

TRY THIS:
Go somewhere you have never been before. This could involve hopping on a bus, a train, or a bike or using your own two feet. Visit a park, a specialty grocery store, a museum, etc.

Prototype + make something!

In UX design there's a mantra: "Fail early, fail fast, fail often." This mantra helps takes the pressure off, lowers the stakes, and leaves perfectionism behind. Too often we want something to be perfect before we put it out into the world. But how will we know if we like something until we try it?

Prototype is a fancy word for TRY. Before we invest too much time, money, energy, or effort, we can cheaply and quickly (think paper, scissors, tape, role playing) discover what works and what doesn't.

Let yourself play. Embrace creative constraints. Regardless of the outcome, each prototype gives us information we can use moving forward. Prototyping is a healthy way to make friends with failure.

TRY THIS:
Without spending money, figure out how you can prototype an idea or try out some aspect of it within the next 24 hours. For another level of creative constraint, do it in 20 minutes or less.

Diversify your bookshelf.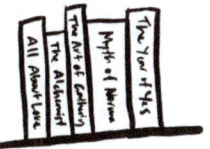

If you look at your bookshelf, who are the authors of the books you read? Are you seeing any trends? At one point I realized the vast majority of books I was reading were by white men, which I conflated with expertise. Without knowing it I was perpetuating a limited way of thinking.

Diversification can include gender, age, race, sexuality, religion, nationality, and socioeconomic, geographic, or educational background. In other words, decolonize your bookshelf. You can also dive into a different genre (for instance, fiction instead of nonfiction) or subject matter. The same idea applies to podcasts, who you follow on social media, or any content you're consuming. Hearing stories and experiences that are different from your own can be eye-opening. Get curious about different ways.

TRY THIS:

Do a mini audit of the books you've read recently (or podcasts you've listened to). What is the breakdown of authors by gender? Who is represented? Who is cited as an expert? Your next challenge is to read or listen to something that represents a different perspective or point of view.

CHANGE THE CHANNEL

**Change the conversation.
Shift the energy.**

WE INTERRUPT THIS PROGRAM

Press pause.

Living in France has taught me the beauty of 5–9 weeks of vacation a year and opened my mind to what it means to take a break. Casper ter Kuile, author of *The Power of Ritual*, has a tech sabbath that starts at the end of the day every Friday. Coach Tiffany Han got me started on my first two-week social media break. My initial resistance transformed into an essential disconnect. It's a good kind of stretch. My favorite gym trainer used to say, "There's no growth without effort."

Often we can find comfort in things that don't always serve us. For some people, it may be scrolling social media; for others it's being hooked to the news, or turning to shopping for a quick fix. Whatever your version is, it's addictive and sucks us in. It's a form of numbing. In a fast-paced world, our need for escape can become an unhealthy distraction, or autopilot where we don't even realize we're doing it. A pause doesn't have to be forever, but it can be a "simple" RESET in our system override.

TRY THIS:
Pick one thing you think you can't go without that may not be serving you and press pause on it. Start with one day. Let it be an experiment. Then go from there.

Monitor your overwhelm meter.

We all can sense when we're getting frustrated or overwhelmed. Instead of hitting pause, the tendency is to keep going—often at all costs. What if we could use this sense of overwhelm as an indicator or warning light?

It may not need to be a full stop but rather putting on the brakes or detouring towards the scenic route. Catch yourself before it becomes too serious, or burnout becomes irreversible, or all the grind pushes you to illness. You can even see it as an opportunity to get creative with your approach.

My overwhelm meter has become an internal indicator to rethink what I'm doing. I feel it in my body, which is an invitation to override my default mode.

← WARNING !
OVER-COMPLICATED.
TIME TO SIMPLIFY.
FOR YOUR SAKE
+ OTHERS'.

Most of the overwhelm comes from societal programming or beliefs around what I should be doing or how I should be operating rather than trusting myself. I've come to learn that I can avoid a lot of headaches and heartache if I pay attention and hit reset. When I'm in my head and spiraling, I can't make a clear decision. In fact, I make things worse.

Recognizing the levels of our personal overwhelm meter is a great way to override the system. It can take some time to recognize what's happening. Pay attention to the way you talk about certain situations (or people), which is often a good indicator that something needs to change.

TRY THIS:

Draw your own overwhelm meter. (It doesn't have to look like mine.) What are the different warning levels? Give them creative names that resonate with you. Keep one visible and train yourself to revisit it at the first sign of stress rising.

Speak your truth.

It may be hard in the moment, but it will always be worth it to speak your truth. Your job is not to make someone else comfortable. Speak your needs. As a child, whenever my mom asked me "How was your day?" my default answer was "fine." How boring! Even if I wasn't fine (which I think I was most of the time), I convinced myself I was. I let the stories I was telling myself run the show rather than being honest.

It's not uncommon to have a default response to questions. Life moves fast and we may feel like we don't want to bother or burden anyone. (The story we tell ourselves . . .) Keeping the facade or false positivity feels easier. We get to a point where we don't realize we're doing it.

You risk a pressure valve exploding if you keep it bottled up. Speaking your truth is not about telling someone else what's wrong with them or blaming others, it's saying how you feel, expressing your needs. It also means being your authentic self and being vulnerable.

TRY THIS:
Watch for moments when you're not telling yourself the truth. Don't be afraid to have a hard conversation.

Go back to the basics.   *H.A.L.T.*

We've all had moments when it feels like everything is falling apart and we're ready to give up. We're so tense and our bodies tighten. They're trying to tell us something.

When we take a deep breath and see what else is going on, we're able to recognize that we'll get through this.

H.A.L.T. is a model in psychology that invites us to ask the simple question: Am I HUNGRY, ANGRY, LONE-LY or TIRED? I also like to throw in two extra H's—hydrated or hormonal—as a way to check in with myself.

This approach has saved me 90% of the time. There's so much that food, water, and even a good night's sleep can solve. Pay attention to what you're consuming (diet- and information-wise) and where you have energy.

TRY THIS:
As soon as you feel overwhelmed, turn to H.A.L.T. and get back to the basics.

Breathe or meditate.

Breathing and meditation are accessible ways to keep us grounded and connected with ourselves and our body, and in turn our intuition. They're tools to bring us back to presence and the power of now, away from the spiral.

Close your eyes. Deep breath in. Deep breath out. Put one hand on your heart and the other on your belly. Take a few deep breaths. Box breathing is another way to slow your breath. Take four counts in. Hold for four counts. Breathe out four counts. Hold for four counts. Repeat.

Meditation, including guided meditation, is another way to focus inward. Don't worry if your mind wanders. Overriding can often be most effective through small, sustainable moments where we can focus on ourselves while supporting our nervous system. These practices are only helpful if you find ways that resonate with you. (There are more tools and approaches in the resources section too.)

TRY THIS:
Take three minutes before bed to breathe. Sit on your bed, close your eyes with your feet grounded on the floor. Put hand on your heart, one on your belly. Let your mind be still.

Take a bath/shower.

Yes, good hygiene is important, but taking a bath or shower can be good for helping us unplug, clear our head, and release tension and unwelcome energy. The simple act also is proof that we're taking a moment of our day for ourselves as we let the water run over us. You'll likely wash away some stress along the way too.

Neurologically, water has connective properties. Chances are you've gotten some great ideas in the shower. My best ideas don't happen at my desk, they happen in the pool (or shower, or making connections in the metro). As soon as we let go of trying to force something to happen, disconnecting our brain and standing under the water can often invite in the flow.

TRY THIS:
Let it flow. Take a bath (add Epsom salts if you have them), shower, or go for a swim. Unplug and enjoy. Repeat any time you feel yourself getting tense for a quick reset.

Create a playlist.

Music is incredibly powerful. It has the power to break the ice, change our mood, recall old memories, spark joy, get us to dance. Hence it's a great tool for shifting the energy or to hype yourself up before a big event, or break a funk. (Don't underestimate the need for silence in our days too.)

My favorite hack for finding flow and getting into the zone is listening to a song on repeat. Do you have a favorite song that makes you feel empowered? Declare it your theme song!

Dance parties are welcome and encouraged too. Dance like nobody's watching. Movement is key when we press override. Invite the joy in while you do. Remember, joy is part of how we override the system!

TRY THIS:
Create your own override playlist. Get creative as you name it. You can create different playlists for different seasons of life, moods, or challenges you're looking to override or overcome. Play on repeat as needed.

PRACTICE

Integration takes time.

Two things can be true at once.

In improv there's a game called "yes, and" where you have to play along with what your partner has said as if the statement were true. I call my version of this the "two truths game," where you name two things that may not go together and agree they can both be true.

Something can be both hard and worth it, or sad and beautiful. "The world is stressful right now AND I can find small ways to invite joy into my life," or "Bureaucracy can be really frustrating AND I'm grateful for the place I call home." The possibilities are endless.

Opening up possibilities beyond the obvious binary is key to overriding. Go beyond the obvious, fixed way of seeing. There are no limits. There are far more than two possible solutions to any scenario, some that we can't see yet.

TRY THIS:
Play your own version of the "two truths game." Remind yourself that conflicting and often opposing ideas can both be valid. Say it out loud to make it feel more true. You can play with multiple truths too.

Define terms.

Just because we speak the same language doesn't mean we understand each other. (Oh, assumptions.) Defining terms allows us to get on the same page. From workplaces and the media, we can get lost in lingo and jargon without backing up to ensure everyone understands what we're actually taking about.

We all bring our ideas based on our own experience and education that can shape, cloud, or even confuse the message. The same term can mean two wildly different things in two different industries. We rarely slow down enough to pause and get clear on what we're actually talking about.

Go for accessible, clear, succinct language when defining terms for maximum clarity. State the "obvious"—then you can discover if it's truly obvious to everyone. Depending on the context, metaphors can be used to get a message across. Defining terms can also be a great tool to realign people (especially if you're onboarding new team members too).

TRY THIS:
What does FUN mean to you? Ask a friend or colleague what it means to them. Discuss.

Storyboard your stories.

When we're stuck in our head, telling ourselves stories, we get blocked in an endless cycle that only perpetuates more of what we're stuck on. We start to see the stories as truths rather than asking, "What if there was another way?"

Storyboarding is a great tool to help us see how a scenario plays out—that's why it's used when making movies, to understand actions and outcomes before going into production. When we make a concept visible, we can see how our mindset shapes the experience, and it becomes a tool to get us unstuck.

For your storyboard, either fold a sheet of paper into six squares or draw lines so you have three boxes on the top and three boxes on the bottom. Each box is like a panel of a comic strip with a drawing (yes, draw! Quick imperfect sketches are what we're going for here) along with a short line of text. The top row of three boxes is going to show us the old story, while the bottom row will reflect the more empowered mindset.

Start in the top left-hand corner with your "old belief"— for instance, "I can't draw"—and write the statement and a visual representation (think stick figures!). In the top middle box, draw what happens when you perpetuate this belief and write a statement that goes with it, such as "therefore I don't draw." In the third box on the top, draw the outcome: "I still can't draw. Therefore, I don't get better."

No need to be an artist here—just capture the idea in a visual form. (Fun fact: Even though I'm a designer, I always told myself I couldn't draw, so I never tried. Fast-forward to now, I love making iPad doodles. People see my work and they have no idea I had this block. In fact, I made all the visuals in this book!)

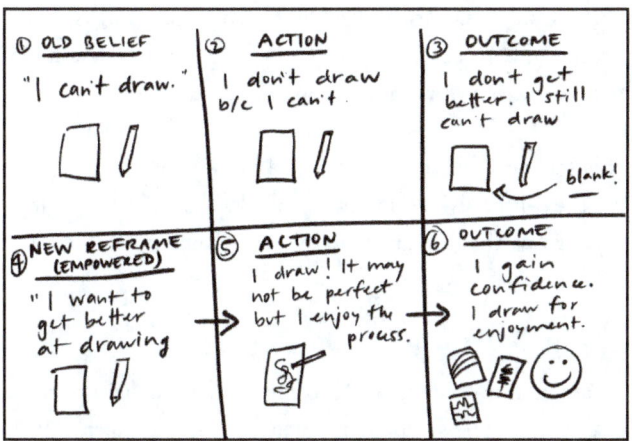

Now you get to revisit the same story on the bottom three boxes, but this time we're going to rewrite the belief, so we can see there's another outcome—there is another way!

The bottom left-hand corner will be a new, more empowered reframe of the original belief you're exploring: "I'm practicing/working on/excited about drawing." In the middle bottom box, now you get to share the new action that is a result of this belief: "I draw a bit every week. It's not perfect, but I enjoy the process." Then in the final box (bottom right), show the new outcome, such as "I'm gaining confidence as an artist!" or "I love drawing for fun!" and maybe there's a big smiley face next to it.

No one wants to hear it, but often we are the biggest hurdle in our own lives. Hence we want to write new narratives that are supportive of how we want to be in the world. Our brains are malleable (see the repetition as reinforcement here). Looking at beliefs is a great way to shift how we see the world and empower ourselves.

This same exercise can be repeated for any belief to help you see—literally—some of the blocks that may be getting in your way that are prime to override. Remember, seeing is believing. Now, take action.

TRY THIS:
Create your own storyboard to explore your belief systems and uncover a new, more supportive thought pattern. Set a timer for 7 minutes so you don't overthink this! Repeat for as many beliefs as you'd like. (Take your time. You don't need to override them all at once.)

Tap into your mind.

Tapping is a somatic technique I learned from my therapist to rewrite neural pathways in order to reprogram more supportive messaging. Now that you've uncovered an empowered belief through reframes and storyboarding beliefs, you can "tap it in" to reinforce new paths in your brain.

Close your eyes and place your feet on the ground. To make a "butterfly hug," cross your arms like an X over your chest. Alternate wrist taps between your left and right shoulder, slowly tapping one and the other. As a variation you can put your hands on your lap and tap the top of your right thigh, then your left thigh, also at a slow rhythm.

As you tap, you want to take the new, supportive belief (e.g., "I am an artist/abundant/loved") and repeat it in your head while you tap. If your mind wanders into negative thoughts, stop tapping until you bring back the empowered belief. Don't stress if you don't fully believe it at first. Repeat daily until the new belief feels integrated.

TRY THIS:
Spend two minutes before bed tapping while thinking of an empowered belief you want to integrate into your life.

Create a new habit, practice, or ritual.

Do you want to move your body more? Dance more? Have more fun? Create more? Bring out your creative or artistic side? Meditate? Walk? Enjoy more time outside? Laugh more? Write more? Do less/nothing? Spend more time reading? Less time on your phone? This all takes intention.

I've come to think of habits in terms of a practice. It takes the pressure off. Consistency is helpful, but I like to give myself the grace of imperfection, knowing I can take a couple days or weeks off and still come back to it. Rituals can be an invitation in. Something as simple as lighting a candle when you start to journal or folding your blanket before bed can help provide moments of peace.

While it can be tempting to want to change everything at once, if you want it to stick, the slow road is often more effective. Don't be hard on yourself—remember the beginner's mind when embracing something new.

Atomic Habits author James Clear says of habits that "Every action you take is a vote for the type of person you wish to become. No single instance will transform your beliefs, but as the votes build up, so does the evidence of your new identity. This is one reason why meaningful change does not require radical change." Real change happens through small steps.

Behavioral scientist B. J. Fogg, through his work *Tiny Habits*, recommends anchoring a new habits to an existing one. My personal favorite is when he suggests flossing one tooth—once you start, you're much more likely to keep going. Set yourself up for success through small actions.

When you reframe what you have to do to something you want to do, it can change everything. I shifted my dread of admin into "Money Mondays," where I check my accounts and follow up on invoices each week. The simple shift and regular interval makes it something I look forward to rather than dread. For me that meant front-loading my week so I could get it out of the way in a way that felt good for me. For someone else it may look completely different.

The key is not forcing habits because you think you're "supposed to" or because society (or some guru) tells you what to do. We all have different ways of working, and we do best when we respond to our own rhythms.

TRY THIS:
Experiment with a habit that supports a real desire that you can do in two minutes or less a day. Keep the stakes low and lower the barrier to entry. If you want added accountability, get an accountability buddy or track your habits.

Ask for help. Accept help.

Asking for help is one of the hardest things many people can do. Much of this is how we are trained and programmed. It took me a long time (and the help of my therapist) to realize asking for help is a sign of strength, not weakness. It can be hard to accept help too; it's not always easy to be receptive to help from others.

It can feel overwhelming to ask for help, or you're so in something you don't even know what help you need. Being clear, specific, and direct can be beneficial to getting what you need. Cut out the dance. Just ask.

While participating in Mapping Your Path, Ashley Usiskin was unexpectedly diagnosed with cancer, a life lesson that taught him a lot about what he calls "the gift of help" (he even turned his experience into a podcast). When you allow someone else to help and support you, it makes the other person feel good too. Everyone benefits.

TRY THIS:
Ask before assuming the outcome. Practice asking for help in a nonserious situation so when the time comes and you really need help, it's not as scary.

Practice gratitude.

When we're feeling down or overwhelmed, gratitude can be a great tool to help override whatever is in our way while reinforcing more supportive neural pathways. It shifts the energy.

Another friend Ashley hooked me on "gratitude hour," a daily practice where at 4 p.m. every day an alarm goes off and you share three things you're grateful for. The best part of this practice is that you can do it alone or you get to invite anyone you're with to participate. I've done it with people of all ages, and a six-year-old loved it so much that he insisted his family continue doing it.

I've come to learn not everyone resonates with the word *gratitude* (particularly those dealing with long-term illnesses). You're welcome to use another word that resonates more with you, such as *appreciate*. This is not toxic positivity.

TRY THIS:
Cook up your own recipe for practicing gratitude. Start your own gratitude hour or make it a dinner ritual. Perhaps you want to write a gratitude journal. Other people I know keep a "gratitude jar" where they write what they're grateful for on small pieces of paper and read them at the end of the year.

Take small(er) steps.

How often have you done something that took less time than you expected? How often have you done something that took more time than you expected?

Every year I send 100+ notes of gratitude around the new year in the mail. It can't be one thing on a to-do list. It's finalizing my map for the year, reaching out to the printer, picking the paper, finding the right envelopes, updating addresses, addressing the envelopes, making sure I have enough ink to address all the cards, getting enough stamps (for different parts of the world), taking them to the post office. It's a process. I love it, but it takes time.

We're often overambitious to a fault. We put one thing on our to-do list only to realize it's actually dozens of smaller tasks. Small steps are another way I think about buffers. Everything I do takes longer than I think, so I'd rather be hyperrealistic that everything takes time from the start.

TRY THIS:
Break tasks down into tiny steps. Celebrate the small steps along the way by adding them to your TA-DONE! list when you've finished each one. Look at that progress!

Celebrate small wins.

Negativity bias means that often the negative things are what we remember (like the one negative review in a sea of glowing ones). It also means we're more likely to see all the things we haven't done rather than all the things we've accomplished. When we can switch our view from what we didn't do to what we did do, we invite in a spirit of abundance rather than scarcity. That's where the possibility lives!

The goal is to reinforce our brain pathways through celebrating our progress, recognizing that progress can look so many different ways. Don't place judgment or value on the size of your wins. Celebrate them all!

We all encounter difficult chapters in life. It's why it's important to celebrate small wins along the way. It's important to take the time to acknowledge the good things that have happened and what we have achieved or accomplished. Not everything we do will have a tangible output, and achievements don't always look like we'd expect. What comes naturally for others may be a big deal for us—celebrate everything. Small wins are actually the big wins.

Soaking in praise and compliments isn't always comfortable, but we need to celebrate ourselves in order to fully give ourselves credit for our awesomeness and all we've overcome in life. We're rewiring the pathways when we take time for this. Celebrate showing up for yourself!

TRY THIS:
Celebrate your wins daily. In Mapping Your Path, we have a whole channel devoted to celebrating small wins. These wins can be anything from making the time to journal to checking in on a friend to going for a walk.

Keep a "shine file" (call it whatever you want) of positive praise, feedback, accomplishments, and hurdles you've overcome. This can be emails, social media exchanges, screenshots, things you've heard people say about you. Add to it regularly. Revisit it on days when you're feeling defeated.

SUPPORT YOURSELF
(This is not selfish!)

Talk to a professional.

We all carry our own shame, blame, and shadow that need to be rewritten, so working with a professional can be a huge support. It is often through the process of speaking through the mess and emotions that we can get to the deeper root causes. A therapist can also be a mirror to help you see your growth. Having someone on your side to listen can be immensely valuable.

Going to therapy and going through the motions is not enough. Insights only get integrated if you take your external learnings and internalize them. Override old blocks with supportive thought patterns through action, one layer at a time.

Honesty is an essential ingredient—with your therapist, and with yourself. Find someone you feel safe and comfortable with. It may take a few tries to find someone who is the right fit. Stay open and consider triangulating modalities to truly integrate what you're learning about yourself.

Therapists come in all varieties. There are different types of therapists according to your needs. CBT (cognitive behavioral therapy) explores a lot of belief systems, EMDR is a rapid eye movement therapy that can help people who have lived through traumatic experiences, somatic therapists help you get in touch with clues your body may hold, and IFS (Internal Family Systems) is parts work to explore what we've been holding on to from our past. Most blocks stem from when we were young, so don't underestimate supporting your inner child.

My real journey of getting honest with myself didn't start until my late thirties, and still I lacked the vocabulary to describe my emotions for years (searching "wheel of emotions" helped a lot). Now it's rare that I have a conversation with a friend or new contact where I don't mention therapy. It's been important to me to normalize the discussion around mental health and that we're all going through something no matter how good our lives may look from the outside. On the other hand, social media accounts from therapists became an added support in my own reeducation and journey of discovery.

It can be easy to want to avoid therapy for the comforts of what you know, or fear of what you may uncover. Yes, there can be some initial discomfort as we unlock different levels of ourselves, but ultimately it can be freeing and liberating.

TRY THIS:
Connect the dots. Journal about something you've been resisting and see if you can find any links to your childhood or belief systems you grew up with that parallel the experience.

Set boundaries.

Boundaries are guardrails to protect your time and energy. They're are an opportunity to step away from people pleasing and societally programmed niceties. Embodiment practitioner Prentice Hemphill describes boundaries as "the distance at which I can love you and me simultaneously."

We live in a world where we're used to getting everything we want (and quickly). Just because someone says something is urgent doesn't mean it actually is. Remember being bored as a kid and having to figure things out on your own? Other people can figure things out too. It doesn't have to be on you to do it all.

Boundaries are necessary to create a space where you can thrive. The desire to be needed and feel valued is real, but we must understand our limits, when to say no, and that we don't have to take on every opportunity that comes our way (that's scarcity), or be the savior for everyone else.

Setting boundaries is one thing, but upholding them is another. We can want to blame others for interrupting us or distracting us, when really we may be the porous sieve allowing distractions or energy drains in. Don't be surprised if others "test" you in the beginning. This is part of your learning curve to help ensure you actually are serious about the boundaries you're setting.

Boundaries need to be articulated clearly if you expect anyone else to honor them. For instance, "please call rather than text," or you don't check work emails after 6 p.m. or on weekends. As Brené Brown says, "clear is kind." How someone responds is not about you.

Like many terms in the therapeutic world, *boundaries* can be misinterpreted and used as a buzzword. Boundaries are not something that can be imposed on others in an attempt to control or dictate their behavior. Boundaries are guidelines and guardrails for ourselves. Sometimes when we model a behavior of how we want to show up in the world, we can help inspire others to do the same. Show them there's another way.

As Nedra Glover Tawwab points out in *Set Boundaries, Find Peace*, "[Boundaries] are like muscles. The more we set them, the easier they become to set and maintain."

TRY THIS:
Look at an area of your life where you find yourself complaining or frustrated. Play with that space and which boundaries you can set and communicate to improve the situation. Start with something simple and achievable that you can actually uphold.

Permission to say no.

When was the last time you used "No" as a complete sentence without overexplaining yourself? It's not a bad word. You don't have to explain. You do not have to justify your choices. You don't have to have a reason. No can bring you closer to your desires. Say YES to what you really want.

Many of us were raised in a "do it all" culture and never knew there could be another way. We often don't realize we're agreeing to everything and saying yes as we're on autopilot. I'm guilty of being wishy-washy and afraid to say no, fearing disappointing others, only to realize that doesn't help anyone.

In her book *The Joy of Saying No*, Natalie Lue reminds us there are often health ramifications when we don't say no. A self-described recovering people pleaser, she says her actions were often an attempt to control and influence the outcome but would later backfire. She reminds us that there are ways to say no without saying no.

TRY THIS:
Say no to something you always say yes to.

Write your own permission slip.

It's often a challenge to allow ourselves to do things differently. When we're not struggling, it can feel like cheating. Societal pressures and programming can make us think things need to be a certain way. We often don't even realize there's another way. We can hold ourselves back waiting for someone else to give us permission when really, it's us needing to give ourselves permission. We need to get out of our own way.

Sometimes we need to write our permission slip to break the rules, do things differently, or serve as a simple reminder.

Below are a collection of permissions. Use any of them, or write your own:

PERMISSION TO DO THINGS DIFFERENTLY.

PERMISSION TO DO THINGS ON YOUR OWN TIME.

PERMISSION TO SAY NO.

PERMISSION TO LEAVE A SITUATION THAT DOESN'T FEEL RIGHT.

PERMISSION TO RELEASE THE NEED FOR VALIDATION.

PERMISSION TO STOP PEOPLE PLEASING.

PERMISSION TO TRUST YOURSELF.

PERMISSION TO BE SELFISH + (RE)PRIORITIZE YOURSELF.

PERMISSION TO SLOW DOWN OR DO LESS.

PERMISSION TO PAUSE. PERMISSION TO BREATHE.

PERMISSION TO BE EXTRA. BE YOURSELF. SPEAK YOUR TRUTH.

PERMISSION TO DO SOMETHING THAT SCARES + EXCITES YOU.

PERMISSION TO DO THE UNEXPECTED.

PERMISSION TO DO THINGS IMPERFECTLY.

PERMISSION TO TAKE THE NEXT SMALLEST ACTION.

PERMISSION TO PLAY + HAVE FUN!

PERMISSION TO DREAM.

[WRITE YOUR OWN]

PERMISSION TO:

PERMISSION TO:

Stop overcomplicating things.

Life is A LOT. Yet sometimes when I dig deeper with friends and clients, I realize there's more to the story. We get blocked and bogged down thinking we need to do all the things (especially when the "experts" tell us to), yet it doesn't feel right to us. Ask yourself, Does it have to be this way? Maybe there really is another way!

Stop overcomplicating things. Engage your own super powers and strengths. Keep using your body as a barometer. You'll feel it in your body and in your mind when you get there. There will be a new lightness. Invite play, exploration, and curiosity as you find another way. Your way.

TRY THIS:
Not everyone will understand what you really need or offer proper support. Ask a trusted friend, family member, mentor, or boss if you can talk through a scenario. Together, see if there's another way to do the thing or take the pressure off. (Chances are they'll find a way to simplify their life too, and at a minimum they'll feel honored to be asked.)

Give yourself some credit.

The feeling of overwhelm is all too easy when we get a new idea or want to change our life—or the world. Keep in mind the desire for change doesn't have to be an all-or-nothing thing. On a personal level, give yourself credit for the work you've already done. Even if you don't have experience in a particular domain, chances are you have skills and experience that are transferable.

It's only when we're kind to ourselves that we can truly override that which is broken around us. When we're hard on ourselves or beat ourselves up over not having done enough or not being good enough, we're only perpetuating the systems and stay stuck in a pattern that we can't break out of. Grace and self-compassion are essential ingredients.

TRY THIS:
Write a (love) letter to yourself. Hype yourself up as if you were writing about your best friend or favorite person. Don't play small or be self-conscious. Own your awesomeness. Allow yourself to shine.

Take a nap!

"Exhaustion will not save us. Rest will." In a culture of doers and achievers, the words of Tricia Hersey, aka The Nap Ministry, offer an alternative stance of rest as a form of rebellion.

How many times in your life could you have made a better decision, thought more clearly, or saved time if you had allowed yourself a break and taken a nap? Kids take naps all the time, and any parent can tell you how whether their child napped or not affects their mood.

Adults are too good at pressing the unsupportive override and pushing through at all costs even when science supports the power of naps and rest.

In her manifesto *Rest as Resistance*, Hersey gives us permission to dream in order to break free from systems of oppression, inspired by writer/activist bell hooks, who saw imagination as essential for liberation. What if we could see naps as an opportunity to dream?

TRY THIS:
Take a nap! (Guilt-free.)

Connect with others.

We're not wired to go through life alone. We're also not warned that friendships may evolve, change, or enter and exit our lives over time as we evolve as humans. When you press override, you are intentionally showing up in the world differently from default modes. Not every friend or family member will understand the choices we make. Our relationships may be tested in the process of overriding our ways. You may find you need space too. Adult friendship can be challenging. Don't be afraid to build your own support system and reach out when you need extra support.

In *The Art of Gathering: How We Meet and Why It Matters*, Priya Parker invites us to rethink how we gather, where purpose is at the center of decision-making as we create meaningful experiences. I once had an impromptu party to toast a rug I unexpectedly bought in Istanbul. We're overriding old ways when we find new ways to connect.

TRY THIS:
Reach out to someone to say hello or to tell a stranger you like their work with no attachment to outcome. Or perhaps you want cook up a fun excuse to gather people. If you can't find a group, start your own.

Invite in MAGIC!

Every year I come up with a "guiding force" (word/phrase/theme) and draw a map of the year ahead alongside the workshop and community I run. (I share all my maps on my Biz Blog on anneditmeyer.com.) I've come to see that the power of doing this work in the company of others expands pathways in ways I never imagined.

In 2022 (the year this book really got in motion), my guiding force for the year was "The magic within you." It was a departure from previous years' themes. In the process it opened up a whole new way of thinking and being. I learned a lot about letting go, being present, following my intuition, and making space for magic.

The "within you piece" was unexpected and taught me a lot about how we already have everything we need within us, even when we feel like we need others to validate us. This internal shift led to seeing more mundane magic and synchronicities, from Street Wisdom to signs and reminders that would pop up around me (I started seeing "love" and hearts daily a year after my mom passed). It opened my eyes to mundane magic that felt like clues to my next steps, bringing more wonder and joy into my life.

I came to discover that magic is all around us, but we have to be tuned in to it to see how we're being supported in unexpected ways. Remember the magic of when you were a kid and the world was an open book for you.

We lose so much energy trying to control every little thing; we lose a lot of magic when we do. Surrender is about letting go of how and when we think things will play out and instead following the flows of life and trusting that things will happen when they need to happen. Spiritual leader Gabrielle Bernstein describes this not as giving up but giving over. In The *Magic of Surrender,* Kute Blackson shares how life unfolds when we follow our internal compass.

For magic to happen, allowing and receiving are also key ingredients. Tina Roth Eisenberg has a DO Lectures talk where she talks about how "trust breeds magic." There is a big element of trust when it comes to override. We need to be receptive to the unexpected—and the magical—to help show us there's another way. Stay open and don't be afraid to invite in the magic.

TRY THIS:

Open your awareness to the present. What magic is right in front of you? Look for the "magical moments," simple pleasures, and synchronicities in your life. (Revisit "Go for a wander" for more ideas.) Capture and celebrate them. The more you notice, the more you'll see. Keep a running list in a notebook or on your phone.

Draw your own override button.

Whenever the world feels too much, you have permission to hit override. Press the button on this page, on the cover of the book, or the one you draw.

It may seem silly to press a piece of paper, but the intention behind it is to change whatever we're doing in favor of a new course of action. It's a physical reminder of our new belief systems as we retrain the neural pathways in our brain. The more you press it, the more these new ways of operating are reinforced. Consistency over time, even with imperfection, is how change takes hold. We are reinforcing the behaviors that signal and reflect how we want to show up in the world.

German American poet Charles Bukowski put it best in saying, "Can you remember who you were, before the world told you who you should be?" Pressing override really is about coming back to ourselves. It's an invitation to our future selves and the world around us that another way is possible.

TRY THIS:

As you find your way back to yourself, draw your own override button. What does it look like? What shape is it? What color is it?

Consider making more of them for you to keep nearby so you're ready to hit override any time you need to come back to who you are. You can even make it the digital background of your phone, or add a physical button to your phone case or journal.

Press it every time you're ready to do something scary, something new, something different, something that supports you and the way you want to show up in the world.

Here's the perfect spot to draw your first override button:

Deep breath.

CLOSING

(This is only the beginning.)

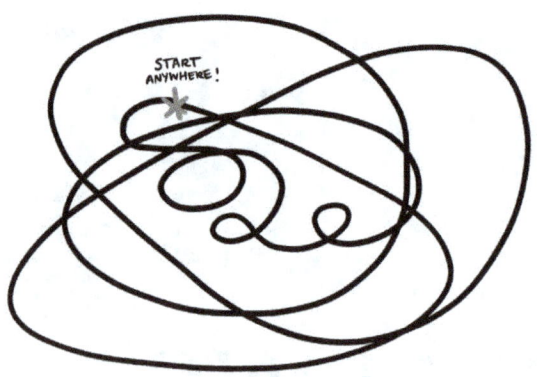

There is another way.

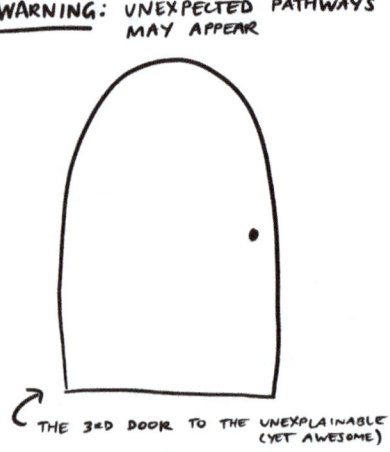

Other ways.

Asking what if there was another way is by no means to suggest there is ONE way to do things, but that there are many possible ways forward that we may not have considered. It may feel tempting to follow the formula of those who claim to have mastered it all, but there is no one way. My way will be different from your way. We all hold answers within us.

Particularly in times of crisis (global or personal) we can feel paralyzed, frozen, lost, angry, sad, heartbroken. How can the world be so hard? So cruel? It can be easy to look at others and be disappointed in their response (or silence).

We all can't respond in the same way, act in the same way, or see the world in the same way. We all have different roles to play that serve not only us but the world at large. The more we stay true to ourselves, the more we're able to bring our own special gifts to the world. A better world is possible where quiet caregivers and healers are just as valuable as vocal activists and figureheads. It's not only the visible leaders making a difference, we all are.

The way forward will rarely look how it has in the past.

The way forward involves imagining a world we may not have seen before. A new vision. Wherever the journey takes us along the way, we must BELIEVE that it's possible. We must also believe in ourselves.

As counterintuitive as it sounds, we need to reprioritize ourselves (yes, put yourself first!) if we're going to be able to make a real contribution. We must care for ourselves if we're going to be able help others.

We engage override in order to embrace our true essence, to come back to ourselves before the world told us who we should be. We have to be ourselves, and sometimes find ourselves along the way. We not only see it but we *feel* it. Our inner gyroscope keeps us centered no matter what comes our way as we build our trust muscles.

It's only when we show up for ourselves that the third door can open—the magical portal that can take us somewhere better than we could have imagined. Set your imagination free. Let's dream a little.

There's always another way.

There's something better out there than you could have imagined. For you, and the world.

Whenever the world feels heavy or hard, turn to your trusty banana map to get out of your head. Bananas are also for dreaming. Now that you've acknowledged what's broken and not working, **it's time to dream.** On a banana.

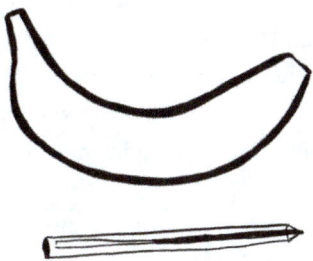

Map your wish for the world on a banana. (Check out https://bit.ly/bananabonus to map with me.) Embrace your inner child—you'll see that a banana is also a smile.

Remember that good kind of contagion? What if a banana map can help start and change the conversation? Capture your banana and share it using #overridebananamap + tag @pretavoyager.

This is only the beginning.

Keep your override button handy. As time passes, hopefully you'll need it less, but know each level you unlock will come with its own challenges. This is exciting. Overriding, rather than defaulting to autopilot, is ultimately how we get back into realignment with ourselves, and with a greater good.

You're well on your way to opening your awareness to the broken systems and what's not working in the world. You know there's another way to see the problem, to ask the question, to connect with others, to view family, to work, to travel, to do anything, to live and enjoy life.

Believing there's another way is an essential step. Don't let outdated beliefs or self-sabotage take you down. Don't try to get anything perfect before you start. Don't get stuck on the how, or the when. Go for what you want even if you don't know the outcome. Believe there's something better than you could imagine. Ignore what others say if it holds you back (if they believe in you, listen—we all need cheerleaders on our side). Believe in yourself.

There are likely times in your life when people have told

you that you can't do something. This may be based on
their own experiences, fears, or programming. You are
your own human. You get to live in the world you want to
live in. You get to choose how you show up in the world
regardless of what is thrown at you. Keep trusting your
intuition and learning to do things your way.

It's OK if your path doesn't look like the paths before us.
The more you live your life on your terms, the more good
will flow and you'll feel aligned.

We have the power to be the change we want to see in the
world, and in ourselves. Delusion or discomfort are not
signals that you're doing anything wrong. You're doing
something right. You're questioning what's no longer working. That's bold. And brave.

Even the smallest actions can be contagious and spread beyond where your eyes can see. Plant the seeds. Give them
space and time, allow them to grow. We're in it for the long
game, not instant gratification. Nurture and water what
you want to see in the world.

Continue to press override against those old and outdated
ways. Sometimes showing up imperfectly is enough. Keep
exploring, stay open, and return to the question: **What if
there was another way?**

Overriding is a lifetime of work, reworking, and refine-
ment. New learnings can serve as redirections. The journey

is the destination, and it's not always linear. Allow it to take the time it takes.

This book is only the beginning. It's not the only way. It's one way. Let it guide you to where you need to go. You have the tools and frames to support you, which you can revisit anytime. On the next read-through, you may want to take on a specific block or challenge.

We can read something or understand a concept, but until we take action, nothing will change. Action is how you integrate and choose other ways. The first step is often the hardest. Keep going. Keep engaging override. Keep showing up for yourself. Keep uprooting old beliefs and patterns. Break the cycle. Ask more questions. Ask better questions. Make way for another way.

You're in the driver's seat. Just like when you miss an exit on the highway and your GPS redirects you, the same can happen in life. You can choose your path. Think of this process as taking the scenic route, where you make new discoveries along the way. You are choosing another way forward.

Return to your internal gyroscope. Usually we learn from experiences for next time, but sometimes it takes a few tries. You can go at your own speed. It's not a race; we can all win. You are not alone. There's no comparison. This is your own journey.

Enjoy the [over]ride!

IT'S NEVER TOO LATE.

THERE'S NO BEHIND.

THIS SHOULD BE <u>FUN</u>!

WHAT IF THERE WAS
ANOTHER WAY?

PLAYGROUND!

What do you want to remember? Capture your thoughts, impressions, insights, and epiphanies each read-through. If you write them on sticky notes, you can see the evolution over time.

Resources

Visit **anneditmeyer.com/override-resources** to find links (follow your curiosity, don't get overwhelmed) and continue the conversation at **override-book.com/conversation.**

MINDSET

Mindset: Changing The Way You Think To Fulfill Your Potential by Dr. Carol S. Dweck

Deepak Chopra's *21 Days of Abundance* meditation podcast

Shinetheory.com or listen to *Call Your Girlfriend*'s "Shine Theory 101 episode"

"Bouncing Back from Rejection" episode of *WorkLife* podcast with Adam Grant

Radically Content: Being Satisfied In An Endlessly Dissatisfied World by Jamie Varon

Brené Brown's TED talk "The Power of Vulnerability," "The Call to Courage" on Netflix; books: *The Gifts of Imperfection, Daring Greatly.*

Playing Big: Find Your Voice, Your Mission, Your Message by Tara Mohr

The Culture Map: Decoding How People Think, Lead, And Get Things Done Across Cultures by Erin Meyer

Everything is Figureoutable by Marie Forleo (which started out as an Oprah talk)

A More Beautiful Question: The Power of Inquiry to Spark Breakthrough Ideas by Warren Berger

DO Listen by Bobette Buster

You Are a Badass at Making Money by Jen Sincero

Lisa Congdon Sessions podcast "Episode 2: Own Your Story" (on imposter syndrome)

"Stop Telling Women They Have Imposter Syndrome" on Harvard Business Review

NEUROSCIENCE

Livewired: The Inside Story Of The Ever Changing Brain by David Eagleman; also featured episode on *Unlocking Us* podcast by Brené Brown

The Source: Open Your Mind. Change Your Life. by neuroscientist and executive coach Dr. Tara Swart Bieber and podcast *Reinvent Yourself* (listen to her episode on *Disrupt Yourself*)

Wired To Create: Unraveling The Mysteries Of The Creative Mind by Carolyn Gregoire and Scott Barry Kaufman

The Biology of Belief by Bruce Lipton

MINDFULNESS + EMBODIMENT

Zen Mind, Beginner's Mind: Informal Talks on Zen Meditation and Practice by Shunryu Suzuki

When Things Fall Apart and *Welcoming the Unwelcome* by Pema Chodron

The Obstacle is the Way by Ryan Holiday

The Creative Act: A Way Of Being by Rick Rubin

Letters from Love with Elizabeth Gilbert elizabethgilbert.substack.com

Finding Our Way podcast by Prentice Hemphill

How We Heal by Alex Elle

We Can Do Hard Things podcast with Glennon Doyle and guest Dr. Hillary McBride, author of *The Wisdom of Your Body: Healing Wholeness, And Connection Through Embodied Living*

Donna Chapman, cofounder of the Conscious Leadership Group on *The Tim Ferriss Show* podcast episode #536 on the "full body yes"

Hell Yeah or No by Derek Sivers

Meditative Story podcast

Breath: The New Science Of A Lost Art by James Nestor

Radical Acceptance and *Radical Compassion* by mindfulness teacher Tara Brach and meditations

Meditation apps: Calm, Insight Timer, Ten Percent Happier, Headspace

MENTAL HEALTH + THERAPY

Search for "wheel of emotions"

Permission to Feel by Marc Brackett, creator How We Feel app for tracking your moods and feelings; Featured on *Unlocking Us* podcast with Brené Brown

Already Enough: A Path To Self-Acceptance by Lisa Olivera

How to Meet Yourself Workbook by Nicole LePerla (Holistic Psychologist online)

The Origins of You: How Breaking Family Patterns Can Liberate the Way We Live and Love by Vienna Pharaon (and *This Keeps Happening* podcast)

"The single most important parenting strategy" TED Talk by Dr. Becky Kennedy + *Good Inside: A Practical Guide To Becoming The Parent You Want To Be* by Becky Kennedy (also good for reparenting oneself)

An Introduction to Internal Family Systems and *No Bad Parts* by Richard C. Schwartz

The Myth of Normal: Trauma, Illness and Healing in a Toxic Culture by Gabor Maté

Homecoming: Overcome Fear And Trauma To Reclaim Your Whole Authentic Self by Dr. Thema Bryant and *Homecoming* podcast

"The Me You Can't See" documentary by Oprah and Prince Harry

"Stutz" Netflix documentary with Jonah Hill's therapist

Man Talks with Connor Beaton podcast

Dr. Kristin Neff's work on self-compassion at self-compassion.org

Nick Ortner of The Tapping Solution (thetappingsolution.com)

The School of Life: An Emotional Education by Alain de Botton

Burnout: The Secret To Unlocking The Stress Cycle by Amelia and Emily Nagoski and guests on *Unlocking Us* with Brené Brown

Please Yourself: How to Stop People-Pleasing and Transform the Way You Live by Emma Reed Turrell (and *Best Friend Therapy* with Elizabeth Day and Emma Reed Turrell)

Codependent No More: How To Stop Controlling by Melody Beattie or listen to her on *We Can Do Hard Things*

"Inside Out" (Pixar film)

"Couples Therapy" show on Showtime

BOUNDARIES

The Joy Of Saying No: A Simple Plan To Stop People Pleasing, Reclaim Boundaries, And Say Yes To The Life You Want by Natalie Lue and her podcast *Baggage Reclaim*

Set Boundaries, Find Peace by Nedra Glover Tawwab (also on *Ten Percent Happier* podcast)

Boundary Boss: The Essential Guide to Talk True, Be Seen, and (Finally) Live Free

by Terri Cole (also on *The Marie Forleo* *podcast*)

The Book Boundaries: Set The Limits That Set You Free by Melissa Urban (also on *Everything Happens with Kate Bowler*)

One Sec app is a tool that can help establish boundaries with social media

HABITS/RITUAL

Atomic Habits: An Easy & Proven Way To Build Good Habits & Break Bad Ones by James Clear (also on *Disrupt Yourself* podcast)

The Power Of Ritual: Turning Everyday Activities Into Soulful Practices by Casper ter Kuile

4,000 Weeks by Oliver Burkeman (listen to him on *Hurry Slowly* podcast)

Hurry Slowly podcast with Jocelyn Glei

I Didn't Do The Thing Today: Letting Go Of Productivity Guilt by Madeleine Dore

Do Pause by Robert Poynton

The Artist's Way by Julia Cameron

BJ Fogg "tiny habits" free five-day program at tinyhabits.com

The High Five Habit by Mel Robbins

Essentialism by Greg McKweon

Indistractable: How to Control Your Attention and Choose Your Life by Nir Eyal

WHEN: The Scientific Secrets Of Perfect Timing by Daniel Pink

Checklist Manifesto by Atul Gawande

This Morning Walk podcast by Libby DeLana and Alex Elle

Keep Going! by Austin Kleon

SOCIAL JUSTICE

Whitesupremacyculture.info

surj.org

Me and White Supremacy by Layla Saad

How to Be an Anti-Racist by Ibram X. Kendi

So You Want to Talk About Race? by Ijeoma Oluo

I'm Still Here: Black Dignity in a World Made for Whiteness by Austin Channing Brown

"13th" [2016 documentary]

Project Inkblot's "Designing for Diversity" on The Creative Independent

Rachel Cargle and The Great Unlearn

Antionette Carroll, The Creative Reaction Lab (crxlab.org)

SOCIETAL SHIFTS

We Can Do Hard Things podcast with Glennon and Amanda Doyle, and Abby Wambach

Rest as Resistance: a manifesto by Tricia Hersey

Ejaculate Responsibly: A Whole New Way To Think About Abortion by Gabrielle Blair

On Our Best Behavior: The Seven Deadly Sins And The Price Women Pay To Be Good by Elise Loehnen and *Pulling the Thread* podcast

This Could Be Our Future by Yancey Strickler

How I Built This podcast with Ben & Jerry, and with Yvon Chouinard

Benandjerrys.com

Professional Troublemaker: The Fear-Fighter Manual by Luvvie Ajayi Jones

How to Change the World by John-Paul Flintoff

Robert Reich (robertreich.org)

The 15 Commitments of Conscious Lead-

ership: *A New Paradigm for Sustainable Success* by Jim Dethmer, Diana Chapman, Kaley Klemp

Winner Takes All: The Elite Charade Of Changing The World by Anand Girihararardas

The Body is Not an Apology: The Power Of Radical Self Love by Sonya Renee Taylor

Emergent Strategy: Shaping Change, Changing Worlds by adrienne marie brown

No One Is Coming To Save Us podcast [on US childcare] with Kristen Bell and Gloria Riviera

Anne Helen Petersen's *Culture Study* newsletter annehelen.substack.com

Deepa Iyer's work, socialchangemap.com

"Barbie" the movie (2023)

CHRONIC ILLNESS

Disability Visibility Project + book (disabilityvisibilityproject.com)

The Invisible Kingdom: Reimagining Chronic Illness by Meghan O'Rourke

Between Two Kingdoms by Suleika Jaoud (also of The Isolation Journals)

Everything Happens For A Reason: And Other Lies I've Loved and *No Cure for Being Human* by Kate Bowler (and her podcast *Everything Happens with Kate Bowler*)

The Gift of Help with Ashley Usiskin podcast

Mismatch: How Inclusion Shapes Design by Kat Holmes

Being Mortal: Medicine And What Matters In The End by Atul Gawande

GRIEF + LOSS

The Modern Loss Handbook: An Interac- tive Guide to Moving Through Grief and Building Your Resilience by Rebecca Soffer (cofounder of modernloss.com)

Alua Arthur, a death doula behind Going with Grace TED talk "Why thinking about death helps you live a better life" (listen to her on *We Can Do Hard Things*)

"We don't 'move on' from grief. We move forward with it" TED talk by Nora McInerny

Final Gifts: Understanding The Special Awareness, Needs, And Communication Of The Dying by Maggie Callanan and Patricia Kelley

Option B by Sheryl Sandberg and Adam Grant

LIFE GUIDANCE

Designing Your Life by Bill Burnett and Dave Evans

Design the Life You Love by Ayse Birsel

How to Fail with Elizabeth Day podcast and book

Life is in the Transitions by Bruce Feiler

The Big Leap by Gay Hendricks

The Heroine's Journey by Maureen Murdock

Reset with Liz Tran podcast

Nancy Sun of Possible Things

On Being podcast by Krista Tippett

ZigZag podcast with Manoush Zomorodi

AWE + WONDER

Wanderful: Human Navigation For A Complex World – Find Wonder In The Everyday. Every Day. by David Pearl

StreetWisdom.org

Play: How It Shapes The Brain, Opens The Imagination, And Invigorates The Soul by Stuart Brown, M.D. with Christopher Vaughan

The Power of Wonder: The Extraordinary Emotion That Will Change the Way You Live, Learn, and Lead by Monica C. Parker

The Art of Noticing: 131 Ways to Spark Creativity, Find Inspiration, and Discover Joy in the Everyday by Rob Walker

"Play your way to joy" TEDx by Roger Manix

The Thrilling New Science of Awe by Dacher Keltner; featured on "On Being" with Krista Tippett

The Power of Fun: How to Feel Alive Again by Catherine Price + "Why Having Fun is the Secret to a Healthier Life" TED Talk

Joyful: The Surprising Power Of Ordinary Things To Create Extra Ordinary Happiness by Ingrid Fetell Lee and "Aesthetics of Joy"

INTUITION + INNER MAGIC

Big Magic by Elizabeth Gilbert

Expanded podcast and To Be Magnetic by Lacy Phillips

Trust Your Vibes: Live An Extraordinary Life By Using Your Intuitive Intelligence by Sonia Choquette and podcast *It's All Related*

A Year of Magical Living with Imogen Roy podcast

The Magic of Surrender by Kute Blackson

The Power of NOW by Eckhart Tolle

The Surrender Experiment by Michael Singer

Speak Your Truth: Connecting With Your Inner Truth And Learning To Find Your Voice by Fearne Cotton

A Return to Love by Marianne Williamson

Vibrate Higher Daily by Lalah Delia

Tina Roth Eisenberg "Trust Breeds Magic" DO Lectures (on YouTube)

The Universe Has Your Back and *Super Attractor* by Gabrielle Bernstein (and the *Dear Gabby* podcast)

Spiritual tools: Lee Harris Energy monthly energy updates, Chani app + podcast, *Embodied Astrology* podcast, The Pattern app

CONNECTION

We Should Get Together: The Secret To Cultivating Better Friendships by Kat Vellos

A Social Life, with Friends podcast by Madeleine Dore

Big Friendship: How We Keep Eachother Close by Aminatou Sow and Ann Friedman

The Art Of Gathering: How We Meet And Why It Matters by Priya Parker

U.S. Surgeon General Vivek Murthy's work around loneliness

The Gottman Institute (on relationships)

Where do we begin podcast with Esther Perel

Just Enough Research by Erika Hall

COMFORT

Wintering by Katherine May and *How We Live Now* podcast

The Comfort Book by Matt Haig

All About Love: New Visions by bell hooks

WRITE YOUR FAVORITE GO-TO RESOURCES FOR EASY REFERENCE:

In gratitude

Thank you to the endless inspiration I receive through books, articles, podcasts, newsletters, blogs, and conversations with friends, collaborators, and clients. So many of these ideas have shaped my writing. I've done my best to point to sources and credit where I can. At times an idea roots in my subconscious and I don't always know where it came from, or someone else shared it through their lens.

Writing a book takes a village. Below is an incomplete list of influences and supports, some of whom I know, some of whom have no idea who I am. In no particular order:

Mister Rogers, Miss Frizzle, To Be Magnetic, Lacy Phillips, Jessica Gill, Lee Harris Energy, Gabby Bernstein, Glennon Doyle, Abby Wambach, Amanda Doyle, Liz Gilbert, Ayse Birsel, Austin Kelon, Julia Cameron, Sonia Choquette (and Sonia and Sabrina Tully), John Gottman and Julie Schwartz Gottman (The Gottman Institute), Shonda Rhimes, Antionette Carroll (and the Creative Reaction Lab), Tara Mohr, Renée Sells, Brené Brown, Priya Parker, Adam Grant, Kat Vellos, Dr. Thema Bryant, Dolly Parton, Vienna Pharaon, Jamie Varon, Jillian Reilly, Karden Rabin, Jocelyn Glei, Chani Nicholas, Ted Lasso,

Rebecca Welton, Derek Sivers, Rick Rubin, Tiffany Han, Imogen Roy, Jen Carrington, Paul Sockett, Paco de Leon, Deesha Dyer, Natalie Lue, Lauren O'Neill, Graham Tomlinson, Emily Reese, Catherine Taret, Camille Sereis, Meg Gagnard + Hugo, Laurel Nock, Pat Petriello, Larissa De Villa, Caitlin Hawekotte, Caitlin Earley, Felice Q. Cleveland, Rachel Hazell, Robin Davis, Shweta Trivedi, Karen Ward, Zoya Draper, Andre Lavergne, Oliver and Lina Gee, Samuél Lopez-Barrantes, Augusta Sagnelli, Jay Swanson, Emily Gaudichon, Deanna White, Katie Mitchell, Jane Bertch, Cécile Poignant, Judith de Graaff, Kate Hill, Nicole de Beaufort, Lauren Gibson, Roger Manix, David Pearl, Brannan Sirratt, Nicole Janz, Laurie Mucha, Silvano Stagni, Matt Trinetti, Parul Bavishi, London Writers Salon (the community, gold coaches, and writers), Alliance of Independent Authors, Tim at Lulu, Joanna Penn, Tina Roth Eisenberg and the Creative Mornings Team, Phil Francis (the originator of banana maps in my first Skillshare course), my therapist, my family, my amazing friends, my wonderful clients, my beta readers, and everyone who has ever signed up for any of my workshops.

TAKE A MOMENT FOR YOUR OWN GRATITUDE.

It's always a pleasure to hear from readers and hear how this book may have touched you or someone in your life.

Thank you for your support! Please tell your friends.

About the author

Anne S. Ditmeyer is a Paris-based designer turned writer, creative coach, and workshop facilitator who is American by birth and French by hard work. She's not one to take the standard path and invites the question "What if there was another way?" in all of her work.

Through her creative workshops Write Your Own Rules and Mapping Your Path, she loves guiding a global community, giving them the confidence to get lost and explore the world in creative ways. She's known to make people map on bananas.

Author photo: Katie Mitchell Photography

anneditmeyer.com
override-book.com
@pretavoyager

ANOTHER WAY PRESS empowers readers to see the world through a different lens, and change the world while you're at it.

Learn more about my workshops Write Your Own Rules and Mapping Your Path at anneditmeyer.com/workshops

BONUS MINI WORKSHOP. BRING A BANANA :)

(PRESS THIS BUTTON ANY
TIME YOU NEED A RESET
OR TO CHANGE YOUR
DEFAULT WAYS.)

Tell your friends!
override-book.com